Ivor Cutler

(20th)

Signed by poet ↑

£2·50

The Phoenix Anthologies

HUMOROUS VERSE

Humorous Verse

AN ANTHOLOGY CHOSEN BY

E. V. KNOX

1950

Chatto & Windus

LONDON

First issued in the Phoenix Library
First publication 1931
Reprinted 1932, 1939
This edition 1950

Preface

MORE, if possible, than others, this anthology may seem pleasantly remarkable for what it omits. Pleasantly, because the reader, it seems to me, has a twofold advantage here. He has the joy of attacking the compiler, and he has the secret relief of not discovering all that he knows and fears.

Whilst many very well-known pieces have of course been included in this collection, it has on the whole been ruthlessly made. With but few exceptions, I have left out what I may be pardoned for calling ancient light verse. Modern convention demands so much technique and polish in this kind of writing that the old, set side by side with it, seems cruder than it is, and suffers unfairly by comparison. It is to Horace-worship in the eighteenth century and still more to Horace-worship in the nineteenth century that we owe the diligent neatness of our modern humorous verse : there is a divergence also (but this is less Horatian) in themes. The subject-matter which provided rough fun to our forefathers would be the inspiration to-day of picaresque romance. We take a serious pride in our larger vices, and do not dismiss them in uproarious rhymes. We are also sentimentalists. Even the death of one so humble as a carrier would not call into action with us, as it did with John Milton, what he might have called the unbuskined Muse. Nor could we find as much humour as Gay found in the motion of an apple-woman's head bouncing along the frozen Thames. When a modern verse-writer deals with misery and disaster, he does so paradoxically, catastrophically, and there is no doubt that he cannot mean what he says. Plenty of fun is made out of death in this anthology, but it is neither grim nor gentle fun : it is sheer topsyturvydom.

This humane consideration permits me to use the nursery horrors of Max Adeler and Captain Harry Graham, whilst ruling out Tom Hood's ballad of *Faithless Nelly Gray*. Hood was a reactionary about the humour of decease.

I have left out parodies. There are many reasons for this, but the most important is that the best parodies are often those that amuse the fewest readers, and vice versa. In any case, they are criticisms of literature, and not of life. And if, as is almost inevitable, there have slipped in one or two examples of this kind of verse, there are none, I hope, which have not a more general application, so that they can be regarded as mere outbursts of gaiety, apart from their imitative style.

I have left out songs. There are too many thousands of these, and the pleasure lies too far in the singing. It may be objected that several of the pieces which are included have certainly been set to music and sung. It will be objected also that many songs are amusing in themselves. To these objections I can think at the moment of no adequate reply. But I have left out songs.

I have left out verses for children, except, as I have previously indicated, those in which children suffer so violently and terribly that no sensitive child—perhaps—will care to read them. The kind of verse which enters with sympathy and tenderness into the child's mind would seem a *genre* of its own.

Writers of humorous verse as a whole seem to make a dead set against the very young.

Largely, too, I have excluded light verse about animals, of which it might be possible to form an immense library to-day. It is a curious characteristic of our age that animals, wild or tame, elicit so much melody. I say this notwithstanding Catullus and other well-known exemplars. There is probably no kind of dog or cat, amongst all the many breeds of cats and dogs, about which I could not have discovered a hymn of praise during lifetime or a threnody after death. And the same may be said of the tiger, the rhinoceros, the ant-eater, and a host of other specimens which, preserved in the Zoological Gardens, delight us during the term of their captivity. There are also birds.

I have not adhered rigidly to this rule and there will be found in this book a very small section devoted, and without unkindness, to dogs. But if I had not exercised a certain austerity in this matter I should have had to dedicate the entire collection to the Kennel Club.

I have left out, for the most part, satire and epigram where the intention has been to wound and not to please. They are not to be distinguished with propriety from serious verse. Yet I am glad to think that many satirical and even savagely cynical pieces have forced their way, by some happy chance, through my barriers.

Lastly, I have excluded a great mass of excellent light verse which is playful rather than amusing. This has been much the most difficult line to draw, and I can scarcely pretend that I have achieved it with any firmness of touch. In the main I have followed the principle that in each case the writer should have made a deliberate attempt to amuse, and not merely chosen a trivial subject and discussed it in metrical form. Quantities of good verse are daily and weekly written on themes which die stillborn.

What then remains ? I venture to think, a great deal of excellent comedy, with not too limited a range. I have classified the verse that broke through my fences not according to its authors, nor its dates, but according to the subject-matter, in the hope that what is lost in pedantry may be gained in pleasure, and if any one subject—as, for instance, the subject of love, or family life—seems to overbalance the others, this may be due to a general tendency on the part of light-verse writers or to some predilection of my own. Not even in a humorous anthology can one escape from Freud.

I should have concluded my preface here, but I remember that one omission, perhaps the most serious of all, remains unchronicled. It has been my experience, whenever I have sought for counsel on light verse, that the friend to whom I have been speaking has said :

" The best light verse that was ever written was done by Robinson-Smith "—(or some such name).

" And where," I have asked, " is it to be found ? "

" It has never been republished," he replied. " It was in the pages of an old college magazine, or the *Wigan Times*."

" But Robinson-Smith himself may have copies of those numbers ? " I pursued eagerly.

" Very likely. The worst of it is, he is in Ecuador."

" But I might write to him ? "

" I doubt it. No one has heard of his address for some six or seven years."

Unfortunate. Yet I cannot doubt that my adviser has been telling the truth. However it may be, none of the verses of Robinson-Smith have been included in this volume. The name of nearly every author whose work (or play) is represented here is well known. From some of them I should like to have borrowed half that they have written. All of them, living or dead, have been to me, while I made the book, excellent company, and I hope they will prove so, collected here, to others.

E. V. K.

Acknowledgment

THE Editor wishes to express his sincere thanks to the following authors for permission to include their poems: Mr. Hilaire Belloc, Mr. E. C. Bentley, Mr. C. H. Bretherton, Mr. J. K. Chalmers, Mr. G. K. Chesterton, Captain Harry Graham, Mr. C. L. Graves, Mr. F. Anstey Guthrie, Mr. A. P. Herbert, Major John Kendall, Father R. A. Knox, Mr. E. V. Lucas, Mr. A. A. Milne, Mr. J. B. Morton, Mr. Alfred Noyes, Sir A. Quiller Couch, Sir Owen Seaman, Mr. Humbert Wolfe; and to the following publishers and other owners of copyright for permission to quote from the books here mentioned: *Messrs. George Allen and Unwin*, Threnody, from *The Path to Rome*, by Hilaire Belloc. *Messrs. Edward Arnold & Co.*, D and F from *A Moral Alphabet*, by Hilaire Belloc; The Stern Parent, Mr. Jones, from *Ruthless Rhymes*, by Captain Harry Graham. *Messrs. Ernest Benn, Ltd.*, Why Doesn't She Come? Nanny, from *She Shanties*, by A. P. Herbert; The Proletariat, from *Plain Jane*, by A. P. Herbert; The Poodle and the Pug, from *Ballads for Broadbrows*, by A. P. Herbert; The Rhyme of the Stout Men in October, from *Poems of Impudence*, by E. V. Knox; A Spider and a Fly, Cheerio my Deario, from *Archy and Mehitabel*, by Don Marquis; Two Sparrows, from *Kensington Gardens*, by Humbert Wolfe; The Taungs Man, from *Lampoons*, by Humbert Wolfe. *Messrs. G. Bell & Sons*, Ode on a Distant Prospect of Making a Fortune, Precious Stones, First Love, Companions, On the Beach, Morning, from *Fly Leaves*, by C. S. Calverley. *Messrs. Basil Blackwell & Mott, Ltd.*, The Seventh Hole, The Contented Bachelor, from *The Seventh Hole*, by Major Kendall. *Messrs. Wm. Blackwood & Sons, Ltd.*, The Massacre of the Macpherson, My Wife's Cousin, from the *Bon Gaultier Ballads*; Ode to the Nightingale, from *Oh, Helicon*, by Major Kendall. *Messrs. Bowes & Bowes*, Oxford Revisited, from *The Muse in Motley*, by Hartley Carrick. *Messrs. Bowes & Bowes and Sir Herbert Stephen*, Malines, To R. K., from *Lapsus Calami*, by J. K. Stephen. *Messrs. Bradbury & Agnew, Ltd.*, for the poems by Shirley Brooks, J. K. Chalmers, C. L. Graves,

A. P. Herbert, Major Kendall, E. V. Knox, R. C. Lehmann, A. A. Milne, Sir Owen Seaman—all first published in *Punch*. Messrs. *Cassell & Co., Ltd.*, The Yellow Room, from *The Return of the Scarecrow*, by Alfred Noyes. Messrs. *Chatto & Windus*, The Aged Pilot Man, from *The Innocents at Home*, by Mark Twain; Plain Language from Truthful James, The Society upon the Stanislaus, The Lost Tails of Miletus, from *Collected Poems of Bret Harte*; Not Quite Fair, from *Carols of Cockayne*, by H. S. Leigh; Blowing from the Urals, from *Blue Feathers*, by E. V. Knox; The Passing of the Strange Guest, from *I'll Tell the World*, by E. V. Knox. Messrs. *Constable & Co.*, Lipton Unlimited, The Literary Parasite, The Schoolmaster Abroad, from *A Harvest of Chaff*, by Sir Owen Seaman; My First Catch, from *A Fool's Paradise*, by Major Kendall. Messrs. *Constable and the Executors of Sir Walter Raleigh*, Of the Nations, by Sir W. Raleigh. Messrs. *Gerald Duckworth*, Lord Finchley, from *More Peers*, by Hilaire Belloc; Godolphin Horne, from *Cautionary Tales*, by Hilaire Belloc; Lines on "England," from *Caliban's Guide to Learning*, by Hilaire Belloc. *The Proprietors of the "Granta,"* Bangkolidye, by Barry Pain. *The Proprietors of the "Graphic,"* Etiquette, by Sir W. S. Gilbert. Messrs. *Macmillan & Co., Ltd., and Lady Gilbert*, The Story of Prince Agib, Peter the Wag, The Bumboat Woman's Story, from *The Bab Ballads*, by Sir W. S. Gilbert; Blue Blood, from *Iolanthe*, in *The Savoy Operas*, by Sir W. S. Gilbert. Messrs. *Macmillan & Co., Ltd.*, A Strange Wild Song, from *Sylvie and Bruno*, by Lewis Carroll. Messrs. *Methuen & Co.*, Burglar Bill, from *The Anstey Omnibus*, by F. Anstey; Noah, The English Road, from *The Flying Inn*, by G. K. Chesterton; The Bath, from *The World We Laugh In*, by Captain Harry Graham; Sons, from *Strained Relations*, by Captain Harry Graham; To an Old Bat, The First Tee, from *Those Were the Days*, by A. A. Milne; The Pekinese National Anthem, by E. V. Lucas. Messrs. *Nelson & Co.*, The Missouri Maiden's Farewell, from *Tom Sawyer*, by Mark Twain. *Oxford University Press*, Graeculus Esuriens, Ad Lectionem Suam, Vernal Verses, Pensées de Noël, from *Lyra Frivola*, by A. D. Godley; The Famous Ballad of the Jubilee Cup, Lady Jane, from *Green Bays*, by Sir A. Quiller Couch. Messrs. *Sheed & Ward*, The Oneness of the Philosopher with Nature, from *Greybeards at Play*, by G. K. Chesterton; Tripe, The Dancing Cabman, from *The Beachcomber Omnibus*,

xii

by J. B. Morton. *Messrs. Sidgwick & Jackson*, The Strenuous Life, by A. H. Sidgwick ; The Little Dog's Day, by Rupert Brooke. *Messrs. Spottiswoode & Co.*, Greek Terminology, from *Signa Severa*, by R. A. Knox. *Messrs. T. Werner Laurie, Ltd.*, Sir Christopher Wren, George Hirst, from *Biography for Beginners*, by E. C. Bentley.

Contents

B

xviii

MADNESS AND MYSTERY

The Story of Prince Agib

STRIKE the concertina's melancholy string !
Blow the spirit-stirring harp like anything !
    Let the piano's martial blast
    Rouse the echoes of the past,
For of AGIB, Prince of Tartary, I sing !

Of AGIB, who, amid Tartaric scenes,
Wrote a lot of ballet-music in his teens :
    His gentle spirit rolls
    In the melody of souls—
Which is pretty, but I don't know what it means.

Of AGIB, who could readily, at sight,
Strum a march upon the loud Theodolite.
    He would diligently play
    On the Zoetrope all day,
And blow the gay Pantechnicon all night.

One winter—I am shaky in my dates—
Came two starving Tartar minstrels to his gates ;
    Oh, Allah be obeyed,
    How infernally they played !
I remember that they called themselves the
    " Oüaits."

Oh ! that day of sorrow, misery, and rage,
I shall carry to the Catacombs of Age,
    Photographically lined
    On the tablet of my mind,
When a yesterday has faded from its page !

3

Alas ! PRINCE AGIB went and asked them in ;
Gave them beer, and eggs, and sweets, and scent,
    and tin ;
   And when (as snobs would say)
   They had " Put it all away,"
He requested them to tune up and begin.

Though its icy horrors chill you to the core,
I will tell you what I never told before—
   The consequences true
   Of that awful interview,
For I listened at the keyhole in the door !

They played him a sonata—let me see !
" *Medulla oblongata* "—key of G.
   Then they began to sing
   That extremely lovely thing,
" *Scherzando ! ma non troppo, ppp.*"

He gave them money, more than they could count,
Scent from a most ingenious little fount,
   More beer in little kegs,
   Many dozen hard-boiled eggs,
And goodies to a fabulous amount.

Now follows the dim horror of my tale,
And I feel I'm growing gradually pale ;
   For even at this day,
   Though its sting has passed away,
When I venture to remember it, I quail !

The elder of the brothers gave a squeal.
All-overish it made me for to feel.
   " O Prince," he says, says he,
   " *If a Prince indeed you be,*
I've a mystery I'm going to reveal !

4

" Oh, listen, if you'd shun a horrid death,
To what the gent who's speaking to you saith :
  No ' Oüaits ' in truth are we,
  As you fancy that we be,
For (ter-remble !) I am ALECK—this is BETH ! '

Said AGIB, " Oh ! accursed of your kind,
I have heard that ye are men of evil mind ! "
  BETH gave a dreadful shriek—
  But before he'd time to speak
I was mercilessly collared from behind.

In number ten or twelve, or even more,
They fastened me, full length, upon the floor.
  On my face extended flat,
  I was walloped with a cat,
For listening at the keyhole of a door.

Oh ! the horror of that agonizing thrill !
(I can feel the place in frosty weather still.)
  For a week from ten to four
  I was fastened to the floor,
While a mercenary wopped me with a will !

They branded me and broke me on a wheel,
And they left me in an hospital to heal ;
  And, upon my solemn word,
  I have never, never heard
What those Tartars had determined to reveal.

But that day of sorrow, misery, and rage,
I shall carry to the Catacombs of Age,
  Photographically lined
  On the tablet of my mind,
When a yesterday has faded from its page !

                SIR W. S. GILBERT.

He thought he saw an Elephant
 That practised on a fife :
He looked again, and found it was
 A letter from his wife.
" At length I realize," he said,
 " The bitterness of Life ! "

He thought he saw a Buffalo
 Upon the chimney-piece :
He looked again, and found it was
 His Sister's Husband's Niece.
" Unless you leave this house," he said,
 " I'll send for the police ! "

He thought he saw a Rattlesnake
 That questioned him in Greek :
He looked again, and found it was
 The Middle of Next Week.
" The one thing I regret," he said,
 " Is that it cannot speak ! "

He thought he saw a Banker's Clerk
 Descending from the bus :
He looked again, and found it was
 A Hippopotamus :
" If this should stay to dine," he said,
 " There won't be much for us ! "

He thought he saw a Kangaroo
 That worked a Coffee-mill :
He looked again, and found it was
 A Vegetable-Pill.
" Were I to swallow this," he said,
 " I should be very ill ! "

6

He thought he saw a Coach-and-Four
    That stood beside his bed :
He looked again, and found it was
    A Bear without a Head.
" Poor thing," he said, " poor silly thing .
    It's waiting to be fed ! "

LEWIS CARROLL.

The Nutcrackers and the Sugar-Tongs

(From Edward Lear's "Nonsense Rhymes," published by Messrs. Frederick Warne & Co.)

I

THE Nutcrackers sate by a plate on the table,
    The Sugar-tongs sate by a plate at his side ;
And the Nutcrackers said, " Don't you wish we were able
    " Along the blue hills and green meadows to ride ?
" Must we drag on this stupid existence for ever,
    " So idle and weary, so full of remorse,—
" While every one else takes his pleasure, and never
    " Seems happy unless he is riding a horse ?

II

" Don't you think we could ride without being instructed ?
    " Without any saddle, or bridle, or spur ?
" Our legs are so long, and so aptly constructed,
    " I'm sure that an accident could not occur.
" Let us all of a sudden hop down from the table,
    " And hustle downstairs, and each jump on a horse !

7

" Shall we try ? Shall we go ? Do you think we
    are able ? "
The   Sugar-tongs   answered   distinctly, " Of
    course ! "

III

So down the long staircase they hopped in a minute,
    The Sugar-tongs snapped, and the Crackers said,
        " Crack ! "
The stable was open, the horses were in it ;
    Each took out a pony, and jumped on his back.
The Cat in a fright scrambled out of the doorway,
    The Mice tumbled out of a bundle of hay,
The brown and white Rats, and the black ones from
        Norway,
    Screamed out, " They are taking the horses away ! "

IV

The whole of the household was filled with amaze-
        ment,
    The Cups and the Saucers danced madly about,
The Plates and the Dishes looked out of the case-
        ment,
    The Saltcellar stood on his head with a shout,
The Spoons with a clatter looked out of the lattice,
    The Mustard-pot climbed up the Gooseberry Pies,
The Soup-ladle peeped through a heap of Veal Patties,
    And squeaked with a ladle-like scream of surprise.

V

The Frying-pan said, " It's an awful delusion ! "
    The Tea-kettle hissed and grew black in the face ;
And they all rushed downstairs in the wildest con-
        fusion,
    To see the great Nutcracker-Sugar-tong race.

8

And out of the stable, with screamings and laughter
 (Their ponies were cream-coloured, speckled with
   brown),
The Nutcrackers first, and the Sugar-tongs after,
 Rode all round the yard, and then all round the
  town.

VI

They rode through the street, and they rode by the
 station,
 They galloped away to the beautiful shore ;
In silence they rode, and " made no observation,"
 Save this : " We will never go back any more ! "
And still you might hear, till they rode out of hearing,
 The Sugar-tongs snap, and the Crackers say
  " Crack ! "
Till far in the distance, their forms disappearing,
 They faded away.—And they never came back !
EDWARD LEAR.

A "Prize" Poem

FULL many a gem of purest ray serene,
That to be hated needs but to be seen,
Invites my lays ; be present sylvan maids,
And graceful deer reposing in the shades.

I am the Morning and the Evening Star,
Drag the slow barge, or wheel the rapid car
While wrapped in fire the realms of ether glow,
Or private dirt in public virtue throw.

How small of all that human hearts endure
The short and simple annals of the poor !
I would commend their bodies to the rack ;
At least we'll die with harness on our back !

Remote, unfriended, melancholy, slow,
Virtue alone is happiness below !
As vipers sting, though dead, by some review ;
And now thou seest my soul's angelic hue.

SHIRLEY BROOKS.

Greek Terminology

WHENEVER they speak of abolishing Greek, its
  defenders employ the apology,
That a chemistry " pro " is expected to know the
  details of Greek terminology ;
But why should we use the absurd P's and Q's the
  pedant invented of yore ?
How sweet to the ears are the praises of Ceres, and
  to speak of her daughter as Core !

No longer we smile at the mention of Phyle ; no
  longer the pedagogue writhes,
When we tell him of Chloe, and the volatile Zoe,
  and the weird appellation of Scythes ;
But the nymph Galatea is a rhyme for the sea, and
  a fleet is commanded by Chares ;
And the double address of Ἄρες Ἄρες is lost in
  the compromise Ares.

Why shouldn't Lalage (as a rhyme to le Sage) be a
  prominent star of the ballet,
Or (if Helena marries a person called Paris) the
  brother of Zetes be Calais ?
Or a process converse will perhaps intersperse (it is
  purely a matter of choice)
Tollemache sage, and Descartes the mage, and Tele-
  phone's silvery voice.

10

Oh, pine for the day when professors will say that
    they are not admirers of Goethe,
When Æneas parades the meadows of Hades. and
    walks by the waters of Lethe,
When our tutor dilates on *fidus Achates* (for the tree
    is discerned by its fruits),
And the brave Menelaus, and the beauty of Glauce,
    and the waxing and waning of Bootes.

R. A. KNOX.

The Yellow Room

THE Princess lolls at ease,
    Among forgotten sins.
A dragon clasps her knees.
    A Queen with forty chins
Looks down at her. *Chinese.*

The bed is like a bun,
    (So full of little crumbs)
That she can never sleep).
    The kettle hums and hums
And hums. *Uriah Heep.*

O humming-bird of brass,
    Where have we met before?
The sunset, like an ass,
    Neighs through the open door.
What of her eye-balls? *Glass.*

Nebuchadnezzar knew
    Those chins in other days.
The Fourth Dimension, too,
    Is bulging through her stays.
Where *did* we meet? *The zoo.*

ALFRED NOYES.

The Turnip Crier

IF the man who turnips cries,
Cry not when his father dies,
'Tis a proof that he had rather
Have a turnip than his father.

SAMUEL JOHNSON.

The Lost Tails of Miletus

HIGH on the Thracian hills, half hid in the billows of
    clover,
Thyme, and the asphodel blooms, and lulled by
    Pactolian streamlet,
She of Miletus lay, and beside her an aged satyr
Scratched his ear with hoof, and playfully mumbled
    his chestnuts.

Vainly the Maenid and the Bassarid gambolled about
    her,
The free-eyed Bacchante sang, and Pan—the re-
    nowned, the accomplished—
Executed his difficult solo. In vain were their
    gambols and dances ;
High o'er the Thracian hills rose the voice of the
    shepherdess wailing.

" Ai ! for the fleecy flocks,—the meek-nosed, the
    passionless faces ;
Ai ! for the tallow-scented, the straight-tailed, the
    high-stepping ;
Ai ! for the timid glance, which is that which the
    rustic, sagacious,
Applies to him who loves but may not declare his
    passion ! "

Her then Zeus answered slow : " O daughter of
    song and sorrow,—
Hapless tender of sheep,—arise from thy long lamen-
    tation !
Since thou canst not trust fate, nor behave as
    becomes a Greek maiden,
Look and behold thy sheep."—And lo ! they returned
    to her tailless !

BRET HARTE.

Enigma

'TWAS whispered in Heaven, 'twas muttered in Hell,
And echo caught softly the sound as it fell :
In the confines of earth 'twas permitted to rest,
And the depth of the ocean its presence confessed ;
'Twas seen in the lightning, 'twas heard in the
    thunder,
'Twill be found in the spheres when they're riven
    asunder ;
'Twas given to man with his earliest breath,
It assists at his birth and attends him in death,
Presides o'er his happiness, honour, and health,
'Tis the prop of his house and the end of his wealth ;
It begins every hope, every wish it must bound,
With the husbandman toils, and with monarchs is
    crowned ;
In the heaps of the miser 'tis hoarded with care,
But is sure to be lost in the prodigal heir ;
Without it the soldier and sailor may roam,
But woe to the wretch who expels it from home ;
In the whispers of conscience it there will be
    found,
Nor e'er in the whirlwind of passion be drowned ;

It softens the heart, and though deaf to the ear,
It will make it acutely and instantly hear ;
But in shades let it rest, like an elegant flower,
Oh ! breathe on it softly, it dies in an hour.

C. M. FANSHAWE.

The Dancing Cabman

ALONE on the lawn
  The cabman dances ;
In the dew of dawn
  He kicks and prances.
His bowler is set
  On his bullet head.
For his boots are wet,
  And his aunt is dead.
There on the lawn,
  As the light advances,
On the tide of the dawn,
  The cabman dances.

Swift and strong
  As a garden roller,
He dances along
  In his little bowler,
Skimming the lawn
  With royal grace,
The dew of the dawn
  On his great red face.
To fairy flutes,
  As the light advances,
In square black boots
  The cabman dances.

J. B. MORTON.

14

WOMAN

Song

Pious Selinda goes to prayers,
  If I but ask a favour;
And yet the tender fool's in tears,
  When she believes I'll leave her.

Would I were free from this restraint,
  Or else had hope to win her!
Would she could make of me a saint,
  Or I of her a sinner!

WILLIAM CONGREVE.

Phyllis's Age

How old may Phyllis be, you ask,
  Whose beauty thus all hearts engages?
To answer is no easy task;
  For she has really two ages.

Stiff in brocade, and pinch'd in stays,
  Her patches, paint, and jewels on;
All day let envy view her face;
  And Phyllis is but twenty-one.

Paint, patches, jewels laid aside,
  At night astronomers agree,
The evening has the day belied;
  And Phyllis is some forty-three.

MATTHEW PRIOR.

No Fault in Women

No fault in women, to refuse
The offer which they most would choose.
No fault in women, to confess
How tedious they are in their dress ;
No fault in women, to lay on
The tincture of vermilion,
And there to give the cheek a dye
Of white, where Nature doth deny.
No fault in women, to make show
Of largeness, when they've nothing so ;
When, true it is, the outside swells
With inward buckram, little else.
No fault in women, though they be
But seldom from suspicion free ;
No fault in womankind at all,
If they but slip, and never fall.

ROBERT HERRICK.

A Gentle Echo on Woman

In the Doric Manner

SHEPHERD. Echo, I ween, will in the wood reply,
And quaintly answer questions : shall I try ?
ECHO.   Try.
SHEPHERD. What must we do our passion to ex-
press ?
ECHO.   Press.
SHEPHERD. How shall I please her, who ne'er loved
before ?
ECHO.   Be Fore.
18

SHEPHERD. What moves women when we them
address ?

ECHO. A dress.

SHEPHERD. Say, what can keep her chaste whom I
adore ?

ECHO. A door.

SHEPHERD. If music softens rocks, love tunes my
lyre.

ECHO. Liar.

SHEPHERD. Then teach me, Echo, how shall I come
by her ?

ECHO. Buy her.

SHEPHERD. When bought, no question I shall be
her dear ?

ECHO. Her deer.

SHEPHERD. But deer have horns : how must I keep
her under ?

ECHO. Keep her under.

SHEPHERD. But what can glad me when she's laid
on bier ?

ECHO. Beer.

SHEPHERD. What must I do when women will be kind ?

ECHO. Be kind.

SHEPHERD. What must I do when women will be
cross ?

ECHO. Be cross.

SHEPHERD. Lord, what is she that can so turn and
wind ?

ECHO. Wind.

SHEPHERD. If she be wind, what stills her when she
blows ?

ECHO. Blows.

SHEPHERD. But if she bang again, still should I
bang her ?

ECHO. Bang her.

SHEPHERD.   Is there no way to moderate her anger?
ECHO.   Hang her.
SHEPHERD.   Thanks, gentle Echo! right thy answers
        tell
    What woman is and how to guard her well.
ECHO.   Guard her well.

                                    DEAN SWIFT.

Cheerio my Deario

(By Archy the Cockroach)

WELL boss i met
mehitabel the cat
trying to dig a
frozen lamb chop
out of a snow
drift the other day

a heluva comedown
that is for me archy
she says a few
brief centuries
ago one of old
king
tut
ankh
amen s favorite
queens and today
the village scavenger
but wotthehell
archy wotthehell
it s cheerio
my deario that
pulls a lady through

20

see here mehitabel
i said i thought
you told me that
it was cleopatra
you used to be
before you
transmigrated into
the carcase of a cat
where do you get
this tut
ankh
amen stuff
question mark

i was several
ladies my little
insect says she
being cleopatra was
only an incident
in my career
and i was always getting
the rough end of it
always being
misunderstood by some
strait laced
prune faced bunch
of prissy mouthed
sisters of uncharity
the things that
have been said
about me archy
exclamation point

and all simply
because i was a
live dame

the palaces i have
been kicked out of
in my time
exclamation point

but wotthehell
little archy wot
thehell
it s cheerio
my deario
that pulls a
lady through
exclamation point

framed archy always
framed that is the
story of all my lives
no chance for a dame
with the anvil chorus
if she shows a little
motion it seems to
me only yesterday
that the luxor local
number one of
the ladies axe
association got me in
dutch with king tut and
he slipped me the
sarcophagus always my
luck yesterday an empress
and today too
emaciated to interest
a vivisectionist but
toujours gai archy

toujours gai and always
a lady in spite of hell
and transmigration
once a queen
archy
period

one of her
feet was frozen
but on the other three
she began to caper and
dance singing it s
cheerio my deario
that pulls a lady
through her morals may
have been mislaid somewhere
in the centuries boss but
i admire her spirit

                    archy
                    DON MARQUIS.

A NEW RELIGION

The Latest Decalogue

THOU shalt have one God only; who
Would be at the expense of two?
No graven images may be
Worshipped, except the currency :
Swear not at all; for, for thy curse
Thine enemy is none the worse:
At church on Sunday to attend
Will serve to keep the world thy friend:
Honour thy parents; that is, all
From whom advancement may befall:
Thou shalt not kill; but need'st not strive
Officiously to keep alive:
Do not adultery commit;
Advantage rarely comes of it:
Thou shalt not steal; an empty feat,
When it's so lucrative to cheat:
Bear not false witness; let the lie
Have time on its own wings to fly:
Thou shalt not covet, but tradition
Approves all forms of competition.

A. H. CLOUGH.

IV

WIVES

My Wife's Cousin

DECKED with shoes of blackest polish,
   And with shirt as white as snow,
After matutinal breakfast
   To my daily desk I go ;
First a fond salute bestowing
   On my Mary's ruby lips,
Which, perchance, may be rewarded
   With a pair of playful nips.

All day long across the ledger
   Still my patient pen I drive,
Thinking what a feast awaits me
   In my happy home at five ;
In my small one-storeyed Eden,
   Where my wife awaits my coming,
And our solitary handmaid
   Mutton-chops with care is crumbing.

When the clock proclaims my freedom,
   Then my hat I seize and vanish ;
Every trouble from my bosom,
   Every anxious care I banish.
Swiftly brushing o'er the pavement,
   At a furious pace I go,
Till I reach my darling dwelling
   In the wilds of Pimlico.

" Mary, wife, where art thou, dearest ? "
   Thus I cry, while yet afar ;
Ah ! what scent invades my nostrils ?—
   'Tis the smoke of a cigar !

Instantly into the parlour
  Like a maniac I haste,
And I find a young Life-Guardsman,
  With his arm round Mary's waist.
And his other hand is playing
  Most familiarly with hers ;
And I think my Brussels carpet
  Somewhat damaged by his spurs.
" Fire and furies ! what the blazes ? "
  Thus in frenzied wrath I call ;
When my spouse her arms upraises,
  With a most astounding squall.
" Was there ever such a monster,
  Ever such a wretched wife ?
Ah ! how long must I endure it,
  How protract this hateful life ?
All day long, quite unprotected,
  Does he leave his wife at home ;
And she cannot see her cousins,
  Even when they kindly come ! "

Then the young Life-Guardsman, rising,
  Scarce vouchsafes a single word,
But, with look of deadly menace,
  Claps his hand upon his sword ;
And in fear I faintly falter—
  " This your cousin, then he's mine !
Very glad, indeed, to see you,—
  Won't you stop with us, and dine ? "

Won't a ferret suck a rabbit ?—
  As a thing of course he stops ;
And with most voracious swallow
  Walks into my mutton-chops.

In the twinkling of a bed-post
  Is each savoury platter clear,
And he shows uncommon science
  In his estimate of beer.

Half-and-half goes down before him,
  Gurgling from the pewter pot ;
And he moves a counter motion
  For a glass of something hot.
Neither chops nor beer I grudge him,
  Nor a moderate share of goes ;
But I know not why he's always
  Treading upon Mary's toes.

Evermore, when, home returning,
  From the counting-house I come,
Do I find the young Life-Guardsman
  Smoking pipes and drinking rum.
Evermore he stays to dinner,
  Evermore devours my meal ;
For I have a wholesome horror
  Both of powder and of steel.

Yet I know he's Mary's cousin,
  For my only son and heir
Much resembles that young Guardsman,
  With that self-same curly hair ;
But I wish he would not always
  Spoil my carpets with his spurs ;
And I'd rather see his fingers
  In the fire, than touching hers.

                    BON GAULTIER.

The Joys of Marriage

How uneasy is his life,
Who is troubled with a wife!
Be she ne'er so fair or comely,
Be she ne'er so foul or homely,
Be she ne'er so young and toward,
Be she ne'er so old and froward,
Be she kind, with arms enfolding,
Be she cross, and always scolding,
Be she blithe, or melancholy,
Have she wit, or have she folly,
Be she wary, be she squandering,
Be she staid, or be she wandering,
Be she constant, be she fickle,
Be she fire or be she ickle;
Be she pious or ungodly,
Be she chaste or what sounds oddly,
Lastly, be she good or evil,
Be she saint or be she devil,—
Yet uneasy is his life,
Who is married to a wife.

CHARLES COTTON.

V

HISTORICAL INTERLUDES

The English Road

BEFORE the Roman came to Rye or out to Severn strode
The rolling English drunkard made the rolling
  English road,
A reeling road, a rolling road, that rambles round
  the shire ;
And after him the parson ran, the sexton and the
  squire ;
A merry road, a mazy road, and such as we did tread
The night we went to Birmingham by way of Beachy
  Head.

I know no harm of Buonaparte and plenty of the
  Squire,
And for to fight the Frenchman I did not much desire :
But I did bash their baggonets because they came
  arrayed
To straighten out the crooked road an English drunk-
  ard made,
Where you and I went down the lane with ale-mugs
  in our hands,
The night we went to Glastonbury by way of Goodwin
  Sands.

His sins they were forgiven him : or why should
  flowers run
Behind him ; and the hedges all strengthening in
  the sun ?
The wild thing went from left to right and knew not
  which was which,
But the wild rose was above him when they found
  him in the ditch.

37

God pardon us, nor harden us ; we did not see so
    clear
The night we went to Bannockburn by way of
    Brighton Pier.

My friends, we will not go again nor ape an ancient
    rage,
Or stretch the folly of our youth to be the shame of
    age,
But walk with clearer eyes and ears this path that
    wandereth,
And see undrugged in evening light the decent inn of
    death ;
For there is good news yet to hear and fine things to
    be seen
Before we go to Paradise by way of Kensal Green.

G. K. CHESTERTON.

A Jacobite Toast

GOD bless the King !—I mean the Faith's Defender ;
GOD bless (no harm in blessing) the Pretender !
But who Pretender is and who is King,
GOD bless us all !—that's quite another thing.

J. BYROM.

The Crystal Palace

WITH ganial foire
Thransfuse me loyre,
Ye sacred nymphs of Pindus,
The whoile I sing
That wondthrous thing,
The Palace made o' windows !

38

Say, Paxton, truth,
Thou wondthrous youth,
What sthroke of art celistial,
What power was lint
You to invint
This combineetion cristial.

O would before
That Thomas Moore,
Likewoise the late Lord Boyron,
Thim aigles sthrong
Of godlike song,
Cast oi on that cast oiron !

And saw thim walls,
And glittering halls,
Thim rising slendther columns,
Which I, poor pote,
Could not denote,
No, not in twinty vollums.

My Muse's words
Is like the bird's
That roosts beneath the panes there ;
Her wings she spoils
'Gainst them bright toiles,
And cracks her silly brains there.

This Palace tall,
This Cristial Hall,
Which Imperors might covet,
Stands in High Park
Like Noah's Ark,
A rainbow bint above it.

The towers and fanes,
In other scaynes,
The fame of this will undo,
Saint Paul's big doom,
Saint Payther's, Room,
And Dublin's proud Rotundo.

'Tis here that roams,
As well becomes
Her dignitee and stations,
Victoria Great,
And houlds in state
The Congress of the Nations.

W. M. THACKERAY (1851).

Lipton Unlimited

PRIDE of Britannia's element (the Ocean),
  At what incredible expense and pains,
Sir, you have roused to maritime emotion
    The Viking in our veins!

Mixed nature, like the versatile Phœnician,
  Blending with trade the instincts of a tar,
You keep intact that mercantile tradition
    Which made us what we are!

Reared on a fundamental base of tea-leaves,
  Your tower of fortune scales the arduous sky,
Till on the Hook off which your copper keel heaves
    Two Worlds have fixed their Eye.

Not since the heirs of freedom fairly shivered,
  Waiting on Trafalgar's supreme sea-test,
Has England's universal marrow quivered
    With such a strange unrest.

40

With flaming cheeks or else unearthly pallor,
  Our youth, recalling Nelson's brilliant fight,
Couples that Viscount's mention with the valour
    Of Thomas Lipton, Knight.[1]

I have known public men of light and leading,
  Accustomed at ephemeral themes to scoff,
Turn absolutely giddy just with reading
    The pregnant phrase—THEY'RE OFF!

People of irreligious mind, whose nerve is
  Such that they never know when they have sinned,
Gravely perused the Church of England Service
    To find a prayer for wind.

We loathed the breeze too light to lift a feather,
  Longed for the spanking kind which you prefer,
And asked why what is known as *Shamrock* weather
    Seemed never to occur!

Upsprang at last a twenty-knotted blizzard,—
  Lee-rails awash beneath the scudding brine;
And hope pervaded every patriot's gizzard,
    Warming his blood like wine.

Fathers, unused to these nocturnal capers,
  Up perilous suburban chimneys clomb
To see your efforts told by halfpenny papers
    On the recording bomb.

Infants, neglecting early bed and bottle
  To play their part in this historic scene,
Would watch the preconcerted signals mottle
    Old Thames with red and green.

    [1] Subsequently Bart.

41

Sharp envy overtook the moon at rising ;
  A myriad counter-fires usurped the view ;
So many took this chance of advertising
    Their wares as well as you.

From height to answering height the signs went
    streaming,
  From " Hampstead's swarthy moor " to Wrekin's
    pile,
Till " the red glare on Skiddaw " set blaspheming
    " The burghers of Carlisle."

Bear up ! Sir T. ; remember Bruce's spider ;
  Build further *Shamrocks* through the coming years ;
Virtue like yours, though long retirement hide her,
    Ends in the House of Peers !
                SIR OWEN SEAMAN.

Graeculus Esuriens

THERE came a Grecian Admiral to pale Britannia's
    shore—
In Eighteen Ninety-eight he came, and anchored off
    the Nore ;
An ultimatum he despatched (I give the text com-
    plete),
Addressing it " Τῷ Κυρίῳ, the Premier, Downing-
    street."

" Whereas the sons of Liberty with indignation view
The number of dependencies which governed are by
    you—
With Hellas (Freedom's chosen land) we purpose to
    unite
Some part of those dependencies—let's say the Isle
    of Wight."

42

" The Isle of Wight ! " said Parliament, and
    shuddered at the word ;
" Her Majesty's at Osborne, too—of course, the
    thing's absurd ! "
And this response Lord Salisbury eventually gave :
" Such transfers must attended be by difficulties
    grave."

" My orders," said the Admiral, " are positive and
    flat :
I am not in the least deterred by obstacles like
    that :
We're really only acting in the interests of peace :
Expansion is a nation's law—we've aims sublime in
    Greece."

With that Britannia blazed amain with patriotic
    flames !
'They built a hundred ironclads and launched them
    in the Thames :
They girded on their fathers' swords, both com-
    moners and peers ;
They mobilized an Army Corps, and drilled the
    Volunteers !

The Labour Party armed itself, invasion's path to
    bar ;
Truth and the *Daily Chronicle* proclaimed a Righteous
    War ;
Sir William Harcourt stumped the towns that sacred
    fire to fan,
And Mr. Gladstone every day sent telegrams from
    Cannes.

43

But ere they marched to meet the foe and drench
    the land with gore,
Outspake that Grecian Admiral—from somewhere
    near the Nore—
And " Ere," he said, " hostilities are ordered to
    commence,
Just hear a last appeal unto your educated sense :—

" You can't intend," he said, said he, " to turn your
    Maxims on
The race that fought at Salamis, that bled at
    Marathon !
You can't propose with brutal force to drive from
    off your seas
The men of Homer's gifted line—the sons of
    Socrates ! "

Britannia heard the patriot's plea ; she checked her
    murderous plans :
Homer's a name to conjure with, 'mong British
    artisans :
Her Army too, profoundly moved by arguments like
    these,
Said 'e'd be blowed afore 'e'd fight the sons of
    Socrates.

They cast away their fathers' swords, those com-
    moners and peers,—
Demobilized their Army Corps—dismissed their
    Volunteers :
Soft Sentiment o'erthrew the bars that nations dis-
    unite,
And Greece, in Freedom's sacred name, annexed the
    Isle of Wight.

A. D. GODLEY.

44

SUNSHINE AND STORM

E

Morning

'TIS the hour when white-horsed Day
Chases Night her mares away;
When the Gates of Dawn (they say)
   Phœbus opes:
And I gather that the Queen
May be uniformly seen,
Should the weather be serene,
   On the slopes.

When the ploughman, as he goes
Leathern-gaitered o'er the snows,
From his hat and from his nose
   Knocks the ice;
And the panes are frosted o'er,
And the lawn is crisp and hoar,
As has been observed before
   Once or twice.

When arrayed in breastplate red
Sings the robin, for his bread,
On the elmtree that hath shed
   Every leaf;
While, within, the frost benumbs
The still sleepy schoolboy's thumbs,
And in consequence his sums
   Come to grief.

But when breakfast-time hath come,
And he's crunching crust and crumb,
He'll no longer look a glum
   Little dunce:

But be brisk as bees that settle
On a summer rose's petal :
Wherefore, Polly, put the kettle
    On at once.

C. S. CALVERLEY.

Vernal Verses

WHEN early worms began to crawl, and early birds
    to sing,
And frost, and mud, and snow, and rain proclaimed
    the jocund spring,
Its all-pervading influence the Poet's soul obeyed—
He made a song to greet the Spring, and this is what
    he made :—

They sadly lacked enlightenment, our ancestors of
    old,
Who used to suffer simply from an ordinary cold :
But we, of Science's mysteries less ignorant by far,
Have nothing less distinguished than a Bronchial
    Catarrh !

O when your head's a lump of lead and nought can
    do but sneeze :
Whene'er in turn you freeze and burn, and then you
    burn and freeze ;
It does not mean you're going to die, although you
    think you are—
These are the primal symptoms of a Bronchial
    Catarrh.

And when you've taken drugs and pills and stayed
    indoors a week,
Yet still your chest with pain opprest will hardly let
    you speak :
Amid your darksome miseries be this your guiding
    star—
'Tis simply the remainder of a Bronchial Catarrh.

In various ways do various men invite misfortune's
    rods—
Some row within their College boat,—some Logic
    read for Mods :
But oh ! of all the human ills our happiness that
    mar
I do not know the equal of a Bronchial Catarrh !

A. D. GODLEY.

A Reflection

THE heat that has this summer-time
    Such melting moments made—
(But there ! how can a fellow rhyme,
    With eighty in the shade ?)

Ye gods ! it makes the bard desire
    That he in ice be laid :
Far, far too much poetic fire
    Is eighty in the shade.

Shut out the sunlight's scorching smile,
    Call in the punkah's aid !
Here will I lie, and stir not, while
    'Tis eighty in the shade.

A clime so torrid has begun
　　Our island to invade,
Not worse than England in the sun
　　Is Hayti in the shade !

WALTER PARKE

The Rain

THE rain it raineth every day,
　　Upon the just and unjust fellow,
But more upon the just, because
　　The unjust hath the just's umbrella.

ANONYMOUS.

In Winter

BOREAS blows on his high wood whistle,
　　Over the coppice and down the lane
Where the goldfinch chirps from the haulm of the
　　thistle
　　And mangolds gleam in the farmer's wain.
Last year's dead and the new year's sleeping
　　Under its mantle of leaves and snow ;
Earth holds beauty fast in her keeping
　　But Life invincible stirs below.

Runs the sap in each root and rhizome,
　　Primrose yellow and snowdrop cold,
Windyflowers when the chiffchaff flies home,
　　Lenten lilies with crowns of gold.
Soon the woods will be blithe with bracken,
　　April whisper of lambs at play ;
Spring with triumph—and our old black hen
　　(Thank the Lord !) will begin to lay.

C. H. BRETHERTON.

Blowing from the Urals

BLOWING from the Urals, so they say,
The vile East wind comes up this way,
The air is bitter, the earth is grey,
  Dark-blue the nose ;
And banks are broken, and safes are robbed,
And beautiful girls with light hair (bobbed)
Are missing, and referees are mobbed
  When an East wind blows.

Bitter and strange the garden trees,
Solicitors ask for extra fees,
And the milk of kindness turns to cheese
  With an Easterly wind :
And it was on a day like this
That our first father, then in bliss,
Failing to give the fruit a miss,
  Partook and sinned.

Spirits of darkness walk about
And persons hitherto devout
Experience religious doubt,
  Rubber goes down ;
And cats wail on the garden wall,
And income-tax collectors call
And leave their messages in the hall,
  Stamped by the crown.

There is no joy nor any mirth,
But only sorrow over the earth ;
Dresses by Paquin and by Worth
  Lose their appeal ;

On days like these, across the foam
The wild stark Norsemen used to roam :
They must have had poor fun at home
    Is how I feel.

For, crouching over the wood-log fire,
Robbed of all joy and all desire,
Still the vexed Saxon feels with ire
    The window draught ;
Anon he walks into the street
Yellow and writhed, and vultures fleet
Pounce on his liver—that's their meat—
    Both fore and aft.

Blowing from the Urals, so they say,
The vile East wind comes up this way ;
Anyone else can have the day
    When this occurs.
Not all the wool of Persian lambs
Taken from their confounded dams,
Can save my soul, nor all the drams,
    Nor all the furs.

Long marriages end in divorce
When East winds blow, and every horse
Lets down the punter on the course,
    And stockings tear.
Blowing from the Urals, so they say,
The vile East wind comes up this way,
And the world will end upon a day
Bitter as this is, dark and grey—
    But who will care ?

                                E. V. KNOX.

VII

LOVE, COURTSHIP AND ROMANCE

My Fancy

I PAINTED her a gushing thing,
  With years about a score ;
I little thought to find they were
  At least a dozen more ;
My fancy gave her eyes of blue,
  A curly auburn head :
I came to find the blue a green,
  The auburn turned to red.

She boxed my ears this morning,
  They tingled very much ;
I own that I could wish her
  A somewhat lighter touch ;
And if you ask me how
  Her charms might be improved,
I would not have them added to,
  But just a few removed !

She has the bear's ethereal grace,
  The bland hyena's laugh,
The footstep of the elephant,
  The neck of a giraffe ;
I love her still, believe me,
  Though my heart its passion hides ;
" She's all my fancy painted her,"
  But oh ! how much besides !

LEWIS CARROLL.

Advice

Go, thou perpetual whining lover ;
   For shame leave off this humble trade,
'Tis more than time thou gav'st it over,
For sighs and tears will never move her :
   By them more obstinate she's made ;
And thou by Love, fond, constant Love, betray'd.

The more, vain fop, thou su'st unto her,
   The more she does torment thee still ;
Is more perverse the more you woo her ;
When thou art humblest lays thee lower ;
   And, when most prostrate to her will,
Thou meanly begg'st for life, does basely kill.

By Heaven ! 'tis against all nature,
   Honour and manhood, wit and sense,
To let a little female creature
Rule, on the poor account of feature,
   And thy unmanly patience
Monstrous and shameful as her insolence.

Thou may'st find forty will be kinder,
   Or more compassionate at least,
If one will serve, two hours will find her,
And half this do for ever bind her
   As firm and true as thine own breast,
On Love and Virtue's double interest.

But if thou canst not live without her,
   This only she, when it comes to 't,
And she relent not (as I doubt her),

Never make more ado about her,
　To sigh and simper is no boot ;
Go, hang thyself, and that will do't.
CHARLES COTTON.

The Willowy Song

WHEN Fashion said to the girl, " Be slim,"
　And each, in her wonderous way,
Grew slight of body and light of limb,
　And all in a single day ;
When never a flounce or frill was seen,
And never a curve where curves had been,
And the feminine leg (an engrossing member)
　Gave us a long display—

　I gave my heart to the willowy girl ;
　　I said, " She is more my line
　Than the fluffed-out puffed-out billowy girl
　　That yesterday called divine ;
　　I like her slender, I like her light ;
　　The whole effect is exactly right ;
　And I'll take my oath that the pillowy girl
　　Shall never be girl of mine."

And now, when Fashion again has swerved,
　And every girl of taste
Must be well-covered and neatly-curved,
　With signs, I'm told, of a waist ;
When frills and flounces are all the go,
And a mild demeanour is *comme il faut*,
And legs, they say, will be tamely hidden
　By petticoats long and laced—

57

I give my heart to the billowy girl,
　　As a flowery thing to see,
For the dancing prancing willowy girl
　　Is not what a girl should be ;
　　　　If Eve had a figure (as I believe)
　　　　Then all Eve's daughters should be like Eve,
And I feel convinced that the pillowy girl
　　Is really the girl for me.

MAJOR JOHN KENDALL.

"*When Moonlight Ore the Hazure Seas*"

WHEN moonlike ore the hazure seas
　　In soft effulgence swells,
When silver jews and balmy breaze
　　Bend down the Lily's bells ;
When calm and deap, the rosy sleap
　　Has lapt your soal in dreems,
R Hangeline !　R lady mine !
　　Dost thou remember Jeames ?

I mark thee in the Marble All,
　　Where England's loveliest shine—
I say the fairest of them hall
　　Is Lady Hangeline.
My soul, in desolate eclipse,
　　With recollection teems—
And then I hask, with weeping lips,
　　Dost thou remember Jeames ?

Away !　I may not tell thee hall
　　This soughring heart endures—
There is a lonely sperrit-call
　　That Sorrow never cures ;

58

There is a little, little Star,
    That still above me beams ;
It is the Star of Hope—but ar !
    Dost thou remember Jeames ?
W. M. THACKERAY.

The Coquet Mother and the Coquet Daughter

AT the close of the day
When the bean-flower and hay
    Breathed odours in ev'ry wind :
Love enlivened the veins
Of the damsels and swains ;
    Each glance and each action was kind.

Molly, wanton and free,
Kissed, and sat on each knee,
    Fond ecstasy swam in her eyes.
See, thy mother is near,
Hark ! She calls thee to hear
    What age and experience advise.

Hast thou seen the blithe dove
Stretch her neck to her love,
    All glossy with purple and gold ?
If a kiss he obtain
She returns it again :
    What follows, you need not be told.

Look ye, Mother, she cried,
You instruct me in pride,
    And men by good manners are won.
She who trifles with all
Is less likely to fall
Than she who but trifles with one.

59

Prithee, Molly, be wise,
Lest by sudden surprise
   Love should tingle in ev'ry vein :
Take a shepherd for life,
And when once you're a wife,
   You safely may trifle again.

Molly smiling replied,
Then I'll soon be a bride ;
   Old Roger has gold in his chest.
But I thought all you wives
Chose a man for your lives,
   And trifled no more with the rest.

JOHN GAY.

Companions

(A Tale of a Grandfather)

I KNOW not of what we ponder'd
   Or made pretty pretence to talk,
As, her hand within mine, we wander'd
   Tow'rd the pool by the limetree walk,
While the dew fell in showers from the passion flowers
   And the blush-rose bent on her stalk.

I cannot recall her figure :
   Was it regal as Juno's own ?
Or only a trifle bigger
   Than the elves who surround the throne
Of the Fairy Queen, and are seen, I ween,
   By mortals in dreams alone ?

60

What her eyes were like, I know not :
   Perhaps they were blurred with tears ;
And perhaps in your skies there glow not
   (On the contrary) clearer spheres.
No ! as to her eyes I am just as wise
   As you or the cat, my dears.

Her teeth, I presume, were " pearly " :
   But which was she, brunette or blonde ?
Her hair, was it quaintly curly,
   Or straight as a beadle's wand ?
That I fail'd to remark :—it was rather dark
   And shadowy round the pond.

Then the hand that reposed so snugly
   In mine—was it plump or spare ?
Was the countenance fair or ugly ?
   Nay, children, you have me there !
My eyes were p'raps blurred ; and besides I'd heard
   That it's horribly rude to stare.

And I—was I brusque or surly ?
   Or oppressively bland and fond ?
Was I partial to rising early ?
   Or why did we twain abscond,
All breakfastless too, from the public view
   To prowl by a misty pond ?

What pass'd, what was felt or spoken—
   Whether anything pass'd at all—
And whether the heart was broken
   That beat under that shelt'ring shawl—
(If shawl she had on, which I doubt)—has gone,
   Yes, gone from me past recall.

F

Was I haply the lady's suitor?
  Or her uncle? I can't make out—
Ask your governess, dears, or tutor.
  For myself, I'm in hopeless doubt
As to why we were there, who on earth we were,
  And what this is all about.

C. S. CALVERLEY.

"*I'm not a Single Man*"

Lines Written in a Young Lady's Album

A PRETTY task, Miss S—, to ask
  A Benedictine pen,
That cannot quite at freedom write
  Like those of other men.
No lover's plaint my Muse must paint
  To fill this page's span,
But be correct and recollect
  I'm not a single man.

Pray only think, for pen and ink
  How hard to get along,
That may not turn on words that burn
  Or Love, the life of song!
Nine Muses, if I chooses, I
  May woo all in a clan,
But one Miss S— I daren't address—
  I'm not a single man.

Scribblers unwed, with little head
  May eke it out with heart,
And in their lays it often plays
  A rare first-fiddle part.

They make a kiss to rhyme with bliss,
    But if *I* so began,
I have my fears about my ears—
    I'm not a single man.

Upon your cheek I may not speak,
    Nor on your lip be warm,
I must be wise about your eyes,
    And formal with your form ;
Of all that sort of thing, in short,
    On T. H. Bayly's plan,
I must not twine a single line—
    I'm not a single man.

A watchman's part compels my heart
    To keep you off its *beat*,
And I might dare as soon to swear
    At *you*, as at your feet.
I can't expire in passion's fire
    As other poets can—
My life (she's by) won't let me die—
    I'm not a single man.

Shut out from love, denied a dove,
    Forbidden bow and dart,
Without a groan to call my own,
    With neither hand nor heart ;
To Hymen vow'd, and not allow'd
    To flirt e'en with your fan,
Here end, as just a friend, I must—
    I'm not a single man.

                  THOMAS HOOD.

Why Doesn't She Come?

Why doesn't she come?
  I know we said eight.
Or was it half-past?
That clock must be fast.
Why doesn't she come?
  She's ten minutes late.
I'll sit by the door
  And see her come in;
I've brought her a rose,
  I've borrowed a pin.
I'll be very severe,
I'll tell her, " My dear,
You mustn't be late."
It's a quarter past eight.
  Why doesn't she come?

Why doesn't she come?
  This must be the place.
She couldn't forget,
Or is she upset?
Why doesn't she come?
  Am I in disgrace?
Oh, well, if it's that,
We were both in the wrong—
I'll give her the rose
And say I was wrong.
I'll give her a kiss
And tell her I'm sorry—
" I'm *terribly* sorry . . ."
Why doesn't she come?
  Perhaps she is ill—

I fancied last night
Her eyes were too bright—
    A feverish chill?
She's lying in bed,
She's light in the head!
She's dying—she's *dead*!
    Why doesn't she come?

Why doesn't she come?
    She's tired of me—ah?
I've noticed a change;
Last night she looked strange.
So this is the end?
    Why couldn't she say?
Well, never again!
She needn't explain.
I know who it is—
I know who it is!
I've done with her now.
    Why doesn't she come?
Why doesn't she come?
It's nearly half-past.
Well, never again!
I'll send her the rose,
I won't say a word,
Just send her the rose—
She'd *laugh*, I suppose!
A flirt and a fraud!
I'll travel abroad,
I'll go to the East,
I'll shoot a wild beast.
And now for a drink,
I'll have a stiff drink—
A brandy, I think—
    And drown myself in it.

I'll shoot myself. . . .   Oh,
How I love her!—" Hul-*lo*!
What?   *Late?*   Not a minute!"

A. P. HERBERT.

On the Beach

Lines by a Private Tutor

WHEN the young Augustus Edward
Has reluctantly gone bedward
(He's the urchin I am privileged to teach),
   From my left-hand waistcoat pocket
   I extract a batter'd locket
And I commune with it, walking on the beach.

I had often yearn'd for something
That would love me, e'en a dumb thing;
But such happiness seem'd always out of reach:
   Little boys are off like arrows
   With their little spades and barrows,
When they see me bearing down upon the beach;

And although I'm rather handsome,
Tiny babes, when I would dance 'em
On my arm, set up so horrible a screech
   That I pitch them to their nurses
   With (I fear me) mutter'd curses,
And resume my lucubrations on the beach.

And the rabbits won't come nigh me,
And the gulls observe and fly me,
And I doubt, upon my honour, if a leech
   Would stick on me as on others,
   And I know if I had brothers
They would cut me when we met upon the beach.

So at last I bought this trinket.
For (although I love to think it)
'Twasn't *given* me, with a pretty little speech :
No ! I bought it of a pedlar,
Brown and wizen'd as a medlar,
Who was hawking odds and ends about the beach.

But I've managed, very nearly,
To believe that I was dearly
Loved by Somebody, who (blushing like a peach)
Flung it o'er me saying, " Wear it
For my sake "—and I declare, it
Seldom strikes me that I bought it on the beach.

I can see myself revealing
Unsuspected depths of feeling,
As, in tones that half upbraid and half beseech,
I aver with what delight I
Would give anything—my right eye—
For a souvenir of our stroll upon the beach.

O ! that eye that never glisten'd
And that voice to which I've listen'd
But in fancy, how I dote upon them each !
How regardless what o'clock it
Is, I pore upon that locket
Which does not contain her portrait, on the beach !

As if something were inside it
I laboriously hide it,
And a rather pretty sermon you might preach
Upon Fantasy, selecting
For your " instance " the affecting
Tale of me and my proceedings on the beach.

I depict her, ah, how charming !
I portray myself alarming
Her by swearing I would " mount the deadly breach,"
    Or engage in any scrimmage
    For a glimpse of her sweet image,
Or her shadow, or her footprint on the beach.

    And I'm ever ever seeing
    My imaginary Being,
And I'd rather that my marrowbones should bleach
    In the winds, than that a cruel
    Fate should snatch from me the jewel
Which I bought for one and sixpence on the beach.

C. S. CALVERLEY.

Song

Written on the Eve of a Naval Engagement with the Dutch

    To all you ladies now at land
        We men at sea indite ;
    But first would have you understand
        How hard it is to write :
    The Muses now, and Neptune, too,
    We must implore to write to you,
        With a fa, la, la, la, la.

    For though the Muses should prove kind,
        And fill our empty brain :
    Yet if rough Neptune rouse the wind,
        To wave the azure main,
    Our paper, pen, and ink, and we,
    Roll up and down our ships at sea.
        With a fa, la, la, la, la.

Then if we write not by each post,
  Think not we are unkind ;
Nor yet conclude our ships are lost
  By Dutchmen, or by wind :
Our tears we'll send a speedier way,
The tide shall bring 'em twice a day.
    With a fa, la, la, la, la.

The king with wonder and surprise
  Will swear the seas grow bold ;
Because the tides will higher rise,
  Than e'er they used of old :
But let him know it is our tears
Bring floods of grief to Whitehall-stairs.
    With a fa, la, la, la, la.

Should foggy Opdam chance to know
  Our sad and dismal story ;
The Dutch would scorn so weak a foe,
  And quit their fort at Goree ;
For what resistance can they find
From men who've left their hearts behind ?
    With a fa, la, la, la, la.

Let wind and weather do its worst,
  Be you to us but kind ;
Let Dutchmen vapour, Spaniards curse,
  No sorrow we shall find ;
'Tis then no matter how things go,
Or who's our friend, or who's our foe.
    With a fa, la, la, la, la.

To pass our tedious hours away,
  We throw a merry main ;
Or else at serious ombre play ;
  But why should we in vain

Each other's ruin thus pursue ?
We were undone when we left you.
    With a fa, la, la, la, la.

But now our fears tempestuous grow,
    And cast our hopes away,
Whilst you, regardless of our woe,
    Sit careless at a play :
Perhaps permit some happier man
To kiss your hand, or flirt your fan.
    With a fa, la, la, la, la.

When any mournful tune you hear,
    That dies in ev'ry note,
As if it sigh'd with each man's care,
    For being so remote ;
Think then how often love we've made
To you when all those tunes were play'd.
    With a fa, la, la, la, la.

In justice, you can not refuse,
    To think of our distress,
When we for hopes of honour lose
    Our certain happiness ;
All those designs are but to prove
Ourselves more worthy of your love.
    With a fa, la, la, la, la.

And now we've told you all our loves,
    And likewise all our fears ;
In hopes this declaration moves
    Some pity for our tears ;
Let's hear of no inconstancy,
We have too much of that at sea.
    With a fa, la, la, la, la.

            CHARLES SACKVILLE, EARL OF DORSET.

The Sorrows of Werther

WERTHER had a love for Charlotte
  Such as words could never utter ;
Would you know how first he met her ?
  She was cutting bread and butter.

Charlotte was a married lady,
  And a moral man was Werther,
And for all the wealth of Indies,
  Would do nothing for to hurt her.

So he sigh'd and pined and ogled,
  And his passion boil'd and bubbled,
Till he blew his silly brains out,
  And no more was by it troubled.

Charlotte, having seen his body
  Borne before her on a shutter,
Like a well-conducted person,
  Went on cutting bread and butter.

W. M. THACKERAY.

My Old Breeks

MY mither men't my auld breeks,
  An' wow ! but they were duddy,
And sent me to get Mally shod
  At Robin Tamson's smiddy ;
The smiddy stands beside the burn
  That wimples through the clachan,
I never yet gae by the door,
  But aye I fa' a-lauchin'.

duddy] ragged   clachan] village

For Robin was a walthy carle,
  An' had ae bonnie dochter,
Yet ne'er wad let her tak a man,
  Tho' mony lads had socht her ;
But what think ye o' my exploit ?
  The time our mare was shoeing,
I slippit up beside the lass,
  And briskly fell a-wooing.

An' aye she e'ed my auld breeks,
  The time that we sat crackin',
Quo' I, " My lass, ne'er mind the clouts,
  I've new anes for the makin' ;
But gin ye'll just come hame wi' me,
  An' lea'e the carle, your father,
Ye'se get my breeks to keep in trim,
  Myse', an' a' thegither."

" 'Deed, lad, quo' she, " Your offer's fair,
  I really think I'll tak it,
Sae, gang awa', get out the mare,
  We'll baith slip on the back o't :
For gin I wait my father's time,
  I'll wait till I be fifty ;
But na !—I'll marry in my prime,
  An' mak' a wife most thrifty."

Wow ! Robin was an angry man,
  At tyning o' his dochter :
Thro' a' the kintra-side he ran,
  An' far an' near he socht her ;
But when he cam to our fire-end,
  An' fand us baith thegither,
Quo' I, " Gudeman, I've ta'en your bairn,
  An' ye may tak my mither."

crackin'] chattering   clouts] patches   tyning] losing

72

Auld Robin girn'd an' sheuk his pow,
   " Guid sooth ! " quo' he, " Ye're merry,
But I'll just tak ye at your word,
   An' end this hurry-burry."
So Robin an' our auld wife
   Agreed to creep thegither ;
Now, I hae Robin Tamson's pet,
   An' Robin has my mither.

ALEXANDER RODGER.

pow] head

A Song of Impossibilities
(*January*, 1827)

LADY, I loved you all last year,
   How honestly and well—
Alas ! would weary you to hear,
   And torture me to tell ;
I raved beneath the midnight sky,
   I sang beneath the limes—
Orlando in my lunacy,
   And Petrarch in my rhymes.
But all is over ! When the sun
   Dries up the boundless main,
When black is white, false-hearted one,
   I may be yours again !

When passion's early hopes and fears
   Are not derided things ;
When truth is found in falling tears,
   Or faith in golden rings ;
When the dark Fates that rule our way
   Instruct me where they hide
One woman that would ne'er betray,
   One friend that never lied ;

When summer shines without a cloud,
   And bliss without a pain ;
When worth is noticed in a crowd,
   I may be yours again !

When science pours the light of day
   Upon the lords of lands ;
When Huskisson is heard to say
   That Lethbridge understands ;
When wrinkles work their way in youth,
   Or Eldon's in a hurry ;
When lawyers represent the truth,
   Or Mr. Sumner Surrey ;
When aldermen taste eloquence
   Or bricklayers champagne ;
When common law is common sense,
   I may be yours again !

When learned judges play the beau,
   Or learned pigs the tabor ;
When traveller Bankes beats Cicero,
   Or Mr. Bishop Weber ;
When sinking funds discharge a debt,
   Or female hands a bomb ;
When bankrupts study the *Gazette*,
   Or colleges *Tom Thumb* ;
When little fishes learn to speak,
   Or poets not to feign ;
When Dr. Geldart construes Greek,
   I may be yours again !

When Pole and Thornton honour cheques,
   Or Mr. Const a rogue ;
When Jericho's in Middlesex,
   Or minuets in vogue ;

When Highgate goes to Devonport,
  Or fashion to Guildhall ;
When argument is heard at Court,
  Or Mr. Wynn at all ;
When Sidney Smith forgets to jest,
  Or farmers to complain ;
When kings that are are not the best,
  I may be yours again !

When peers from telling money shrink,
  Or monks from telling lies ;
When hydrogen begins to sink,
  Or Grecian scrip to rise ;
When German poets cease to dream,
  Americans to guess ;
When Freedom sheds her holy beam
  On Negroes, and the Press ;
When there is any fear of Rome,
  Or any hope of Spain ;
When Ireland is a happy home,
  I may be yours again !

When you can cancel what has been,
  Or alter what must be,
Or bring once more that vanished scene,
  Those withered joys to me ;
When you can tune the broken lute,
  Or deck the blighted wreath,
Or rear the garden's richest fruit,
  Upon a blasted heath ;
When you can lure the wolf at bay
  Back to his shattered chain,
To-day may then be yesterday—
  I may be yours again !

W. M. PRAED.

Kitty of Coleraine

As beautiful Kitty one morning was tripping,
  With a pitcher of milk from the fair of Coleraine,
When she saw me she stumbled, the pitcher it tumbled,
  And all the sweet butter-milk watered the plain.

O, what shall I do now, 'twas looking at you, now,
  Sure, sure, such a pitcher I'll not meet again,
'Twas the pride of my dairy, O, Barney M'Leary,
  You're sent as a plague to the girls of Coleraine.

I sat down beside her—and gently did chide her,
  That such a misfortune should give her such pain,
A kiss then I gave her—before I did leave her,
  She vowed for such pleasure she'd break it again.

'Twas hay-making season, I can't tell the reason,
  Misfortunes will never come single,—that's plain,
For, very soon after poor Kitty's disaster,
  The devil a pitcher was whole in Coleraine.

E. LYSAGHT.

On Photographs

She played me false, but that's not why
I haven't quite forgiven Di,
    Although I've tried.
This curl was hers, so brown, so bright,
She gave it me one blissful night,
    And—more beside !

In photo we were grouped together
She wore the darling hat and feather
  That I adore ;
In profile by her side I sat
Reading my poetry—but that
  She'd heard before.

Why, after all, Di threw me over
I never knew, and can't discover,
  Or even guess :
Maybe Smith's lyrics she decided
Were sweeter than the sweetest I did—
  I acquiesce.

A week before their wedding-day
When Smith was called in haste away
  To join the Staff,
Di gave to him, with tearful mien,
Our only photograph. I've seen
  That photograph.

I've seen it in Smith's album-book !
Just think ! her hat—her tender look,
  Are now that brute's !
Before she gave it, off she cut
My body, head, and lyrics, but
She was obliged, the little slut,
  To leave my boots.

FREDERICK LOCKER LAMPSON.

Lady Jane

Sapphics

DOWN the green hill-side fro' the castle window
Lady Jane spied Bill Amaranth a-workin';
Day by day watched him go about his ample
        Nursery garden.

Cabbages thriv'd there, wi' a mort o' green-stuff—
Kidney beans, broad beans, onions, tomatoes,
Artichokes, seakale, vegetable marrows,
        Early potatoes.

Lady Jane cared not very much for all these :
What she cared much for was a glimpse o' Willum
Strippin' his brown arms wi' a view to horti-
        Cultural effort.

Little guessed Willum, never extra-vain, that
Up the green hill-side, i' the gloomy castle,
Feminine eyes could so delight to view his
        Noble proportions.

Only one day while, in an innocent mood,
Moppin' his brow ('cos 'twas a trifle sweaty)
With a blue kerchief—lo, he spies a white 'un
        Coyly responding.

Oh, delightsome Love ! Not a jot do *you* care
For the restrictions set on human inter-
-course by cold-blooded social refiners ;
        Nor do I, neither.

Day by day, peepin' fro' behind the bean-sticks,
Willum observed that scrap o' white a-wavin',
Till his hot sighs out-growin' all repression
               Busted his weskit.

Lady Jane's guardian was a haughty Peer, who
Clung to old creeds and had a nasty temper ;
Can we blame Willum that he hardly cared to
               Risk a refusal ?

Year by year found him busy 'mid the bean-sticks,
Wholly uncertain how on earth to take steps.
Thus for eighteen years he beheld the maiden
               Wave fro' her window.

But the nineteenth spring, i' the Castle post-bag,
Came by book-post Bill's catalogue o' seedlings
Mark'd wi' blue ink at " Paragraphs relatin'
               Mainly to Pumpkins."

" W. A. can," so the Lady Jane read,
" Strongly commend that very noble Gourd, the
Lady Jane, first-class medal, ornamental ;
               Grows to a great height."

Scarce a year arter, by the scented hedgerows—
Down the mown hill-side, fro' the castle gateway—
Came a long train and, i' the midst, a black bier,
               Easily shouldered.

" Whose is yon corse that, thus adorned wi' gourd-
          leaves,
Forth ye bear with slow step ? " A mourner answer'd,
" 'Tis the poor clay-cold body Lady Jane grew
               Tired to abide in."

               79

" Delve my grave quick, then, for I die to-morrow.
Delve it one furlong fro' the kidney bean-sticks,
Where I may dream she's goin' on precisely
          As she was used to."

Hardly died Bill when, fro' the Lady Jane's grave,
Crept to his white death-bed a lovely pumpkin :
Clim'd the house wall and over-arched his head wi'
          Billowy verdure.

Simple this tale !—but delicately perfumed
As the sweet roadside honeysuckle. That's why,
Difficult though its metre was to tackle,
          I'm glad I wrote it.
              SIR A. QUILLER-COUCH.

First Love

O MY earliest love, who, ere I number'd
   Ten sweet summers, made my bosom thrill !
Will a swallow—or a swift, or some bird—
   Fly to her and say, I love her still ?

Say my life's a desert drear and arid,
   To its one green spot I aye recur :
Never, never—although three times married—
   Have I cared a jot for aught but her.

No, mine own ! though early forced to leave you,
   Still my heart was there where first we met ;
In those " Lodgings with an ample sea-view,"
   Which were, forty years ago, " To Let."
80

There I saw her first, our landlord's oldest
    Little daughter. On a thing so fair
Thou, O Sun,—who (so they say) beholdest
    Everything,—hast gazed, I tell thee, ne'er.

There she sat—so near me, yet remoter
    Than a star—a blue-eyed bashful imp :
On her lap she held a happy bloater,
    'Twixt her lips a yet more happy shrimp.

And I loved her, and our troth we plighted
    On the morrow by the shingly shore :
In a fortnight to be disunited
    By a bitter fate for evermore.

O my own, my beautiful, my blue-eyed !
    To be young once more, and bite my thumb
At the world and all its cares with you, I'd
    Give no inconsiderable sum.

Hand in hand we tramp'd the golden seaweed,
    Soon as o'er the gray cliff peep'd the dawn :
Side by side, when came the hour for tea, we'd
    Crunch the mottled shrimp and hairy prawn :—

Has she wedded some gigantic shrimper,
    That sweet mite with whom I loved to play ?
Is she girt with babes that whine and whimper,
    That bright being who was always gay ?

Yes—she has at least a dozen wee things !
    Yes—I see her darning corduroys,
Scouring floors, and setting out the tea-things,
    For a howling herd of hungry boys,

In a home that reeks of tar and sperm-oil !
   But at intervals she thinks, I know,
Of those days which we, afar from turmoil,
   Spent together forty years ago.

O my earliest love, still unforgotten,
   With your downcast eyes of dreamy blue !
Never, somehow, could I seem to cotton
   To another as I did to you !

C. S. CALVERLEY.

The Contented Bachelor

WHEN I grow old, if I should live till then—
   As I intend to do—
I hope to be a pattern which all men
   Should wisely keep in view.

I shall not carp or cavil at the lot
   Which lands me with the past ;
It is a fact that, cavilling or not,
   Dash it, it comes at last.

The blithe amusements of one's early prime,
   The bounding and the biff,
Which, if persisted in beyond their time,
   Make one both sore and stiff.

Each in its turn, no doubt, will have to go,
   I hope without a pang ;
I may regret them just a tiny blow,
   But not a serious hang.

82

Late hours, long nights, the chorus and the cup,
  The well-neglected bed,
These too, if I refused to give them up,
  Would give me up instead.

So let them wane. Such joys are of the Spring,
  And, with Spring, let them pass ;
A man who hangs on to that sort of thing
  Too long is but an ass.

And even when the stubborn day shall dawn
  (Alas that this should be !)
When the young maidens are no longer drawn,
  No longer drawn to me—

(May it be far, ye gods, may it be far !
  'Tis solemn fact that I
Have ever been, may I say, popular
  Among the fair and spry)—

Well, I must watch while others have their fling,
  And, though the thought be sad,
If I'm regarded as a dear old thing,
  It may not be so bad.

Thus, even though my lute must own the rift,
  Though time may dim my song,
My pard-like spirit, beautiful and swift,
  Should still go fairly strong.

And so shall I achieve that " soft delight "
  Which years alone can win :
A bright fire and a casement closed at night
  To keep the warm air in.

MAJOR JOHN KENDALL.

VIII

NATURE AND PHILOSOPHY

The Oneness of the Philosopher with Nature

I LOVE to see the little stars
   all dancing to one tune,
I think quite highly of the Sun
   and kindly of the Moon.

The million forests of the Earth
   come trooping in to tea,
the great Niagara waterfall
   is never shy with me.

I am the Tiger's confidant,
   and never mention names :
the Lion drops the formal " Sir,"
   and lets me call him " James."

Into my ear the blushing Whale
   stammers his love. I know
why the Rhinoceros is sad,
   —ah, child ! 'twas long ago.

I am akin to all the Earth
   by many a tribal sign,
the aged pig will often wear
   that sad, sweet smile of mine.

My niece, the Barnacle, has got
   my piercing eyes of black :
the Elephant has got my nose,
   I do not want it back.

I know the strange tale of the Slug :
   the Early Sin—the Fall—
the Sleep—the Vision—and the Vow—
   the Quest—the Crown—the Call.

And I have loved the Octopus
  since we were boys together.
I love the Vulture and the Shark,
  I even love the weather.

I love to bask in sunny fields
  and when that hope is vain,
I go and bask in Baker Street
  all in the pouring rain.

Come snow ! where fly, by some strange law,
  hard snowballs—without noise—
through streets untenanted, except
  by good, unconscious boys.

Come fog ! exultant mystery—
  where, in strange darkness rolled,
the end of my own nose becomes
  a lovely legend old.

Come snow, and hail, and thunderbolts,
  sleet, fire, and general fuss ;
come to my arms, come all at once—
  oh photograph me thus !

G. K. CHESTERTON.

Not Quite Fair

SUMMER and spring the lovely rose,
Unconscious of its beauty, blows—
Condemn'd, in summer and in spring,
To feel no pride at blossoming.

The hills, the meadows, and the lakes,
Enchant not for their own sweet sakes :
They cannot know, they cannot *care*
To know, that they are thought so fair.

The rainbow, sunset, cloud, and star,
Dream not how exquisite they are.
All dainty things of earth and sky
Delight us—but they know not why.

But I—a poet—who possess
The power of loving loveliness,
May ask (and I may ask in vain),
" Why *am* I so intensely plain ? "

H. S. LEIGH.

D

THE Dreadful Dinotherium he
Will have to do his best for D.
The early world observed with awe
His back, indented like a saw.
His look was gay, his voice was strong ;
His tail was neither short nor long ;
His trunk, or elongated nose,
Was not so large as some suppose ;
His teeth, as all the world allows,
Were graminivorous, like a cow's.
He therefore should have wished to pass
Long peaceful nights upon the Grass,
But being mad the brute preferred
To roost in branches, like a bird.[1]
A creature heavier than a whale,
You see at once, could hardly fail
To suffer badly when he slid
And tumbled   (as he always did).
His fossil, therefore, comes to light
All broken up : and serve him right.

[1] We have good reason to suppose
He did so, from his claw-like toes.

Moral.

If you were born to walk the ground,
Remain there ; do not fool around.

HILAIRE BELLOC.

The Taungs Man

HERE lies a man, who was an ape.
Nature, grown weary of his shape,
conceived, and carried out the plan
by which the ape is now the man.

HUMBERT WOLFE.

a spider and a fly

i heard a spider
and a fly arguing
wait said the fly
do not eat me
i serve a great purpose
in the world

you will have to
show me said the spider

i scurry around
gutters and sewers
and garbage cans
said the fly and gather
up the germs of
typhoid influenza
and pneumonia on my feet
and wings

then i carry these germs
into the households of men
and give them diseases
all the people who
have lived the right
sort of life recover
from the diseases
and the old soaks who
have weakened their systems
with liquor and iniquity
succumb it is my mission
to help rid the world
of these wicked persons
i am a vessel of righteousness
scattering seeds of justice
and serving the noblest uses

it is true said the spider
that you are more
useful in a plodding
material sort of way
than i am but i do not
serve the utilitarian deities
i serve the gods of beauty
look at the gossamer webs
i weave they float in the sun
like filaments of song
if you get what i mean
i do not work at anything
i play all the time
i am busy with the stuff
of enchantment and the materials
of fairyland my works
transcend utility
i am the artist

a creator and a demi god
it is ridiculous to suppose
that i should be denied
the food i need in order
to continue to create
beauty i tell you
plainly mister fly it is all
damned nonsense for that food
to rear up on its hind legs
and say it should not be eaten

you have convinced me
said the fly say no more
and shutting all his eyes
he prepared himself for dinner
and yet he said i could
have made out a case
for myself too if i had
had a better line of talk

of course you could said the spider
clutching a sirloin from him
but the end would have been
just the same if neither of
us had spoken at all

boss i am afraid that what
the spider said is true
and it gives me to think
furiously upon the futility
of literature

archy
DON MARQUIS.

IX

SEVERE DISAPPROVAL

Cologne

In Köln, a town of monks and bones,
And pavements fang'd with murderous stones,
And rags, and hags, and hideous wenches ;
I counted two and seventy stenches,
All well defined, and several stinks !
Ye Nymphs that reign o'er sewers and sinks,
The river Rhine, it is well known,
Doth wash your city of Cologne ;
But tell me, Nymphs ! what power divine
Shall henceforth wash the river Rhine ?

S. T. COLERIDGE.

To R. K.

Will there never come a season
Which shall rid us from the curse
Of a prose that knows no reason
And an unmelodious verse :
When the world shall cease to wonder
At the genius of an Ass,
And a boy's eccentric blunder
Shall not bring success to pass ;

When mankind shall be delivered
From the clash of magazines,
And the inkstands shall be shivered
Into countless smithereens,
When there stands a muzzled stripling
Mute, beside a muzzled bore :
When the Rudyards cease from Kipling
And the Haggards ride no more ?

J. K. STEPHEN (1891).

Epitaph on Charles II

HERE lies our Sovereign Lord the King,
    Whose word no man relies on,
Who never said a foolish thing,
    Nor ever did a wise one.

        JOHN WILMOT, EARL OF ROCHESTER.

Of the Nations

A Hymn of Love and Praise

DAMN the Russian
And the Prussian;
Clap a tax on
Every Saxon;
Beat the Gael
With a flail,
What a sot
Is the Scot!
Who says thankee
For the Yankee,
Or has need
Of the Swede,
Or would ask
For the Basque?
That rapscallion
The Italian
Rolls in sin
(Like the Finn).
Men of Spain
Are a bane,
And the French
Yield a stench;
The Chinese

Fail to please,
So perhaps
Do the Lapps.
Good men spit on
Celt and Briton,
And abuse
The Hindus.
The Icelander
Is a gander.
Dangers lurk
In the Turk.
May the low
Esquimaux
Go to pot
With the lot!
In Japan a
Bechuana
Finds a devil
On his level.
The Armenian
And the Fenian
And the Swiss
Are amiss.
Let us squelch
All the Welsh,
Not to speak
Of the Greek,
And the Norse
Too, of course.
They are more
Than a bore,
If they fell
Down to hell
With their bibs on,
Praising Ibsen,

Or were sent
By a gent
To the Zoo—
That would do.

SIR WALTER RALEIGH.

Malines

(*Midnight, July 4th,* 1882)

BELGIAN, with cumbrous tread and iron boots
Who in the murky middle of the night
Designing to renew the foul pursuits
In which thy life is passed, ill-favoured wight,
And wishing on the platform to alight
Where thou couldst mingle with thy fellow-brutes
Didst walk the carriage floor (a leprous sight),
As o'er the sky some baleful meteor shoots :
Upon my slippered foot thou didst descend,
Didst rouse me from my slumbers mad with pain,
And laughedst aloud for several minutes' space.
Oh may'st thou suffer tortures without end :
May fiends with glowing pincers rend thy brain,
And beetles batten on thy blackened face !

J. K. STEPHEN.

Pensées De Noël

WHEN the landlord wants the rent
Of your humble tenement ;
When the Christmas bills begin
Daily, hourly pouring in ;
When you pay your gas and poor rate,
Tip the rector, fee the curate,
Let this thought your spirit cheer—
Christmas comes but once a year.

When the man who brings the coal
Claims his customary dole :
When the postman rings and knocks
For his usual Christmas-box :
When you're dunned by half the town
With demands for half-a-crown,—
Think, although they cost you dear,
Christmas comes but once a year.

When you roam from shop to shop,
Seeking, till you nearly drop,
Christmas cards and small donations
For the maw of your relations,
Questing vainly 'mid the heap
For a thing that's nice, and cheap :
Think, and check the rising tear,
Christmas comes but once a year.

Though for three successive days
Business quits her usual ways ;
Though the milkman's voice be dumb ;
Though the paper doesn't come ;
Though you want tobacco, but
Find that all the shops are shut :
Bravely still your sorrows bear—
Christmas comes but once a year.

When mince-pies you can't digest
Join with waits to break your rest :
When, oh when, to crown your woe,
Persons who might better know
Think it needful that you should
Don a gay convivial mood :—

Bear with fortitude and patience
These afflicting dispensations:
Man was born to suffer here:
Christmas comes but once a year.

A. D. GODLEY.

The Literary Parasite

HE lives within the public eye
  Immune from all investigation
Of how he came to occupy
  That eligible habitation;
I hear of no accomplished feat
  From which he takes the rank of writer,
Yet almost everywhere you meet
  The name of Mr. Bertram Blighter.

His novel, 'Neath a Woman's Spell,
  His book of poems, Past Repealing,
Those jeux d'esprit, Half-hours in Hell,
  That trifle, Round my Study Ceiling—
All these are in a harmless vein
  And leave suburban bosoms lighter,
But cannot possibly explain
  The splendid vogue of Bertram Blighter.

No merely adventitious aid
  Helped him to hit the social target;
His early life is lost in shade—
  I think he went to school at Margate;
Cambridge has housed him at the " Bull,"
  And Oxford only at the " Mitre,"
And so the praise is due in full
  To just himself—to Bertram Blighter.

How does he do it ? I respond—
  " By sitting down with men of letters,
' Author,' ' Omarian,' ' Vagabond,'
  He gets confounded with his betters ;
A member of the great O.P.,
  A fixed and resolute first-nighter,
In all accounts of such you see :
  ' We noticed Mr. Bertram Blighter.' "

At what he calls his " five o'clocks "
  You may assist where genii jostle—
The newest Rage in Paradox,
  The final form of Art Apostle ;
His knowledge of his guests is slight
  And theirs of him is something slighter,
Yet virtue in a steady flight
  Streams from them all on Bertram Blighter.

A moon amid refulgent orbs,
  A bee among a bed of roses,
Their light and sweetness he absorbs
  And as his own elsewhere imposes ;
So, swarming up the rungs of fame
  With ever surer grasp and tighter,
He bears his undisputed claim
  To be " the well-known Bertram Blighter."
                    SIR OWEN SEAMAN.

Epigram

  To John I owed great obligation ;
    But John unhappily thought fit
  To publish it to all the nation,
    So John and I are more than quit.
                    MATTHEW PRIOR.

The Last Straw

THOUGH crowds I find invariably madding,
  Obedient to my better half's decree,
I join my family in their annual gadding,
  At some-or-other London by the Sea.
I'd really rather watch the little nippers,
  Play " little cricket " in the London parks,
Instead of seeing multitudes of trippers,
  Indulging in their elemental larks.

I tolerate this scene of constant " beanos,"
  Which does not flow with honey or with milk,
I acquiesce in Pictures or Casinos,
  The plays which feature sinners clad in silk ;
The mixture of the matutinal dippers,
  The contrast of the buxom and the thin ;
But cannot stand the spectacle of trippers,
  Impaling periwinkles with a pin.

I suffer, though not gladly, Angelinas,
  And Edwins, and their manners on the beach ;
Mouth-organs, ukeleles, concertinas,
  Terrors of song, and liberties of speech,
Wide-trousered youths who slop about in slippers,
  Slim girls who wear an everlasting grin,
But no, I cannot bear the sight of trippers,
  Consuming periwinkles with a pin.

I'm growing more accustomed to the shaving
  By decorative damsels of their napes ;
The shingling and the bingling and the waving,
  Of hair that from the razor-blade escapes ;

I do not wage a war on cocktail sippers
    Or those who blend their ginger-beer with gin,
But oh ! I do detest the sight of trippers
    Who eat their periwinkles with a pin.

I give a patient hearing to the prattle
    Of golfers as they re-enact their rounds ;
I listen-in to Breslau or Seattle,
    Unmoved by any oscillating sounds ;
I view with calm the antics of " stick-lippers,"
    Who slither in the dance but never spin ;
But cannot tolerate the sight of trippers
    When devouring periwinkles with a pin.

In fine, I yearn for permanent seclusion
    From lures I've not the courage to eschew ;
From haunts that mainly offer a profusion
    Of sights and shocks and noises that are new ;
Where fish are seldom to be seen, save kippers,
    Where nights and days are given o'er to din ;
AND where I can't escape from meeting trippers
    Who eat their periwinkles with a pin.
                                    C. L. GRAVES.

The — Hotel

IF ever you go to Dolgelley,
    Don't stay at the — HOTEL ;
There's nothing to put in your belly,
    And no-one to answer the bell.
                            THOMAS HUGHES.

X

FOOD AND DRINK

The Mermaid Tavern

SOULS of poets dead and gone,
What Elysium have ye known,
Happy field or mossy cavern,
Choicer than the Mermaid Tavern?
Have ye tippled drink more fine
Than mine host's Canary wine?
Or are fruits of Paradise
Sweeter than those dainty pies
Of venison?   O generous food!
Dressed as though bold Robin Hood
Would, with his Maid Marian,
Sup and bowse from horn and can.

I have heard that on a day
Mine host's sign-board flew away,
Nobody knew whither, till
An astrologer's old quill
To a sheepskin gave the story,
Said he saw you in your glory,
Underneath a new old sign
Sipping beverage divine,
And pledging with contented smack
The Mermaid in the Zodiac!

Souls of poets dead and gone,
What Elysium have ye known,
Happy field or mossy cavern,
Choicer than the Mermaid Tavern?

JOHN KEATS.

I CANNOT eat but little meat ;
  My stomach is not good ;
But sure I think that I can drink
  With him that wears a hood.
Though I go bare, take ye no care,
  I nothing am a-cold ;
I stuff my skin so full within
  Of jolly good ale and old.

    Back and side go bare, go bare ;
      Both foot and hand go cold ;
    But, belly, God send thee good ale enough,
      Whether it be new or old.

I love no roast but a nut-brown toast,
  And a crab laid in the fire ;
And little bread shall do me stead ;
  Much bread I nought desire.
No frost, no snow, no wind, I trow,
  Can hurt me if I wold,
I am so wrapp'd, and thoroughly lapp'd,
  Of jolly good ale and old.

    Back and side go bare, go bare ;
      Both foot and hand go cold ;
    But, belly, God send thee good ale enough,
      Whether it be new or old.

And Tib, my wife, that as her life
  Loveth well good ale to seek,
Full oft drinks she, till ye may see
  The tears run down her cheek :
108

Then doth she troul to meet the bowl,
  Even as a maltworm should,
And saith, "Sweetheart, I took my part
  Of this jolly good ale and old."

  Back and side go bare, go bare ;
    Both foot and hand go cold ;
  But, belly, God send thee good ale enough,
    Whether it be new or old.

Now let them drink till they nod and wink,
  Even as good fellows should do ;
They shall not miss to have the bliss
  Good ale doth bring men to.
And all poor souls that have scour'd bowls,
  Or have them lustily troul'd,
God save the lives of them and their wives,
  Whether they be young or old.

  Back and side go bare, go bare ;
    Both foot and hand go cold ;
  But, belly, God send thee good ale enough,
    Whether it be new or old.

                              JOHN STILL.

The Massacre of The Macpherson

(From the Gaelic)

I

FHAIRSHON swore a feud
  Against the clan M'Tavish ;
Marched into their land
  To murder and to rafish ;

I   109

For he did resolve
  To extirpate the vipers,
With four-and-twenty men
  And five-and-thirty pipers.

But when he had gone
  Half-way down Strath Canaan,
Of his fighting tail
  Just three were remainin'.
They were all he had,
  To back him in ta battle;
All the rest had gone
  Off, to drive ta cattle.

" Fery coot ! " cried Fhairshon,
  " So my clan disgraced is ;
Lads, we'll need to fight,
  Pefore we touch the peasties.
Here's Mhic-Mac-Methusaleh
  Coming wi' his fassals,
Gillies seventy-three,
  And sixty Dhuinéwassails ! "

" Coot tay to you, sir ;
  Are you not ta Fhairshon ?
Was you coming here
  To fisit any person ?
You are a plackguard, sir !
  It is now six hundred
Coot long years, and more,
  Since my glen was plundered."

" Fat is tat you say ?
    Dare you cock your peaver ?
I will teach you, sir,
    Fat is coot pehaviour !
You shall not exist
    For another day more ;
I will shoot you, sir,
    Or stap you with my claymore ! "

" I am fery glad
    To learn what you mention,
Since I can prevent
    Any such intention."
So Mhic-Mac-Methusaleh
    Gave some warlike howls,
Trew his skhian-dhu,
    An' stuck it in his powels.

In this fery way
    Tied ta faliant Fhairshon,
Who was always thought
    A superior person.
Fhairshon had a son,
    Who married Noah's daughter,
And nearly spoiled ta Flood,
    By trinking up ta water.

Which he would have done,
    I at least believe it,
Had ta mixture peen
    Only half Glenlivet.

This is all my tale :
　　Sirs, I hope 'tis new t'ye !
Here's your fery good healths,
　　And tamn ta whusky duty !
BON GAULTIER.

Anacreontick

THE heavens carouse each day a cup,
No wonder Atlas holds her up.
The trees suck up the earth and ground,
And in their brown bowls drink around.
The sea too, whom the salt makes dry,
His greedy thirst to satisfy,
Ten thousand rivers drinks, and then
Grows drunk and casts them up again.
The sun (and who so right as he ?)
Sits up all night to drink the sea.
The moon quaffs up the sun, her brother,
And wishes she could tope another.
Ev'rything fuddles ; then that I,
Is't any reason, should be dry ?
Well, I will be content to thirst,
But too much drink shall make me, first.
JOHN WILMOT, EARL OF ROCHESTER.

A Ballad on Ale

WHILST some in epic strains delight,
Whilst others pastorals invite,
　　As taste or whim prevail ;
Assist me, all ye tuneful Nine,
Support me in the great design,
　　To sing of nappy ale.

Some folks of cyder make a rout,
And cyder's well enough, no doubt,
  When better liquors fail ;
But wine, that's richer, better still,
Ev'n wine itself (deny't who will)
  Must yield to nappy ale.

Rum, brandy, gin with choicest smack
From Holland brought, Batavia arrack,
  All these will nought avail
To cheer a truly British heart,
And lively spirits to impart,
  Like humming, nappy ale.

Oh ! whether thee I closely hug
In honest can, or nut-brown jug,
  Or in the tankard hail ;
In barrel, or in bottle pent,
I give the generous spirit vent,
  Still I may feast on ale.

But chief, when to the cheerful glass
From vessel pure thy streamlets pass
  Then most thy charms prevail ;
Then, then, I'll bet, and take the odds,
That nectar, drink of heathen gods,
  Was poor, compared to ale.

Give me a bumper, fill it up,
See how it sparkles in the cup,
  O how shall I regale !
Can any taste this drink divine,
And then compare rum, brandy, wine,
  Or aught with nappy ale ?

Inspired by thee, the warrior fights,
The lover woos, the poet writes,
    And pens the pleasing tale ;
And still in Britain's isle confessed
Nought animates the patriot's breast
    Like generous, nappy ale.

High Church and Low oft raise a strife,
And oft endanger limb and life,
    Each studious to prevail ;
Yet Whig and Tory opposite
In all things else, do both unite
    In praise of nappy ale.

O blest potation ! still by thee,
And thy companion Liberty,
    Do health and mirth prevail ;
Then let us crown the can, the glass,
And sportive bid the moments pass
    In quaffing nappy ALE.

JOHN GAY.

Tripe

COME, gentle tripe, the hungry carter's joy,
    Drayman's delight, conductor's second course,
Passion and dream of every errand boy,
    Vision of every rogue that holds a horse,
Bane of all titled ladies, bishops' dread,
    Doom of the softly nurtured, peers' despair,
Was it for this the tall Achilles bled,
    For this that Agamemnon tore his hair ?

Was this the food that launched a thousand ships
   And tore the heart of Dido, as she stood
Above the feast, wiping her royal lips,
   And called her love again—was this the food ?

(The answer is, in a sense, no.)

J. B. MORTON.

From "*Audley Court*"

THERE on a slope of orchard, Francis laid
A damask napkin wrought with horse and hound,
Brought out a dusky loaf that smelt of home,
And, half-cut-down, a pasty costly-made,
Where quail and pigeon, lark and leveret lay,
Like fossils of the rock, with golden yolks
Imbedded and injellied ; last, with these,
A flask of cider from his father's vats,
Prime, which I knew ; and so we sat and eat.

ALFRED, LORD TENNYSON.

The Rhyme of the Stout Men in October

OF all the merry months that make
   Mankind with surfeit seedy,
With pies and fruit and simnel cake,
   And currants hard and beady,
     Not Dan December has the zest
     Of this, in golden glory dressed ;
     We count October much the best
Because we are so greedy.

115

O flaming woods and fire-lit house!
  O nappy ale in tankard!
O oyster, pheasant, partridge, grouse,
    Whereto our heart is anchored!
        The moon of all good cheer begins,
        Our plates are stuffed with vitamins,
        Behold, we wave our double chins
    With joyfulness uncankered.

Let others praise, if praise they will,
  The new potato season,
Asparagus is none so ill,
    We natheless call it treason
        To hymn the loveliness gone by
        When sweetest celery is nigh,
        And Kentish nuts and damson pie—
    Ho, waiter! Set the cheese on.

Ambition, 'tis but idle dust—
  That truth will bear repeating,
And love will fade with age—it must;
    Come then, my pretty sweeting,
        Consult with me the bill of fare,
        Just press the end of yonder pear,
        They seem to have some nice jugged hare—
    One can't go wrong with eating.

Of all the months, serene, severe,
  Gay-hued, or drab and sober,
Of all the months that build the year,
    That robe her or disrobe her,
        October is the month for us,
        The absolutely gluttonous,
        Whose waist is now an overplus!
    Then here's to thee, October!

                                    E. V. KNOX.

Noah

OLD Noah he had an ostrich farm and fowls on the
    largest scale,
He ate his soup with a ladle in an egg-cup big as a
    pail,
And the soup he took was Elephant Soup and the
    fish he took was Whale,
But they all were small to the cellar he took when he
    set out to sail,
    And Noah he often said to his wife when he sat
        down to dine,
    " I don't care where the water gets if it doesn't
        get into the wine."

The cataract of the cliff of heaven fell blinding off
    the brink
As if it would wash the stars away as suds go down
    a sink,
The seven heavens came roaring down for the throats
    of hell to drink,
And Noah he cocked his eye and said, " It looks like
    rain, I think,
    The water has drowned the Matterhorn as deep as
        a Mendip mine,
    But I don't care where the water gets if it doesn't
        get into the wine."

But Noah he sinned, and we have sinned : on tipsy
    feet we trod,
Till a great big black teetotaller was sent to us for
    a rod,

And you can't get wine at a P.S.A., or chapel, or
    Eisteddfod,
For the Curse of Water has come again because of
    the wrath of God,
    And water is on the Bishop's board and the Higher
        Thinker's shrine,
    But I don't care where the water gets if it doesn't
        get into the wine.

G. K. CHESTERTON.

XI

POETRY EXPOSED

Two Poets

I KNEW a poet once; as poets go
He was a most companionable man;
And oft with me, who have no lyric art
And cannot call a regiment of rhymes
To serve my purpose as a poet can,
He proved his skill and built his palace of song,
Rhyme set on rhyme and verse on gleaming verse,
And towers of music gay with flaunting flags,
So that I marvelled, saying, " If for me,
Who have no music, he can thus disclose
His high majestical and airy notes,
How will it be if he should chance to meet
Another poet tuneful as himself ?
Then surely Swinburne will be left behind
And Milton be out-Miltoned; Shakespeare's self
Will own a rival, and the Mermaid Inn
With all its coruscations be revived."
So did I reason, and one day it chanced
As I had hoped—he met a second poet;
And these two talked, and I myself was there
And heard the talk, and thereupon went home
And wrote it down, and this is how it ran :
FIRST POET. Yes, that's a very comfortable chair,
    And so is this ; the cushion fits your back,
    And you can stretch your legs. I like to stretch
    My legs. It seems to make digestion work.
SECOND POET. If my digestion could be got to work
    But half as well as yours I'd not complain ;
    You've tamed your gastric juices.
FIRST POET.   Yes, I've done
    My best to tame them. Have a cigarette ?

SECOND POET. Thanks. Yes, I've got a match.
  Oh blank the thing !
  Its head broke off and burnt me—
FIRST POET.   It's a way
  These wooden matches have. Here, try another,
  Or better, light your cigarette from mine.
SECOND POET. Puff, puff—I've got it, thanks,—
  puff—puff—puff—thanks.
  Where do you get your cigarettes ? This one
  Is really excellent ; one always likes
  To know the latest man for cigarettes.
FIRST POET. I'm glad you like them. I have
  always smoked
  This special size. I get them in Soho
  From Boxley—he is quite a little man,
  But only sells the best. I buy them there
  In lots of half a thousand at a time.
SECOND POET. Thanks. Let me write it down.
  Soho, you said ?
FIRST POET. Church Street, Soho, and Boxley is
  the name.
  I quite forget the number, but you can't
  Mistake the shop.
SECOND POET.   I'll order some to-morrow.
FIRST POET. Mention my name ; he's sure to treat
  you well.
SECOND POET. Thanks. It's a very long time since
  I've been
  In Soho, but I used to know it well,
  With all its funny little restaurants.
FIRST POET. Things change so quickly, don't they ?
SECOND POET.   Yes, they do.
  London's much altered since I was a boy.
FIRST POET. That's very true ; it's hard to find
  one's way.

122

The County Council's pulling all things down,
And what with taxi-cab and motor-bus
It's not too safe to walk in London now.
SECOND POET. No, that it's not ; however, there
  it is.

Such was the talk of these two poet friends.
There was much else, but the above will serve
To show the working of their mighty minds.

R. C. LEHMANN.

Two Sparrows

Two sparrows, feeding,
heard a thrush
sing to the dawn.
The first said " Tush !

In all my life
I never heard
a more affected
singing-bird."

The second said
" It's you and me,
who slave to keep
the likes of he."

" And if we cared,"
both sparrows said,
" we'd do that singing
on our head."

The thrush pecked sideways,
and was dumb.
" And now," they screamed,
" he's pinched our crumb."

HUMBERT WOLFE.

Poeta Fit, Non Nascitur

" How shall I be a poet ?
How shall I write in rhyme ?
You told me once the very wish
Partook of the sublime :
Then tell me how. Don't put me off
With your ' another time.' "

The old man smiled to see him,
To hear his sudden sally ;
He liked the lad to speak his mind
Enthusiastically,
And thought, " There's no hum-drum in him,
Nor any shilly-shally."

" And would you be a poet
Before you've been to school ?
Ah well ! I hardly thought you
So absolute a fool.
First learn to be spasmodic—
A very simple rule.

" For first you write a sentence,
And then you chop it small !
Then mix the bits, and sort them out
Just as they chance to fall :
The order of the phrases makes
No difference at all.

124

" Then, if you'd be impressive,
    Remember what I say,
That abstract qualities begin
    With capitals alway :
The True, the Good, the Beautiful,
    These are the things that pay !

" Next, when you are describing
    A shape, or sound, or tint ;
Don't state the matter plainly,
    But put it in a hint ;
And learn to look at all things
    With a sort of mental squint."

" For instance, if I wished, Sir,
    Of mutton-pies to tell,
Should I say ' Dreams of fleecy flocks
    Pent in a wheaten cell ' ? "
" Why, yes," the old man said : " that phrase
    Would answer very well.

" Then, fourthly, there are epithets
    That suit with any word—
As well as Harvey's Reading Sauce
    With fish, or flesh, or bird—
Of these ' wild,' ' lonely,' ' weary,' ' strange,'
    Are much to be preferred."

" And will it do, O will it do
    To take them in a lump—
As ' the wild man went his weary way
    To a strange and lonely pump ' ? "
" Nay, nay ! You must not hastily
    To such conclusions jump.

K

" Such epithets, like pepper,
    Give zest to what you write,
And, if you strew them sparely,
    They whet the appetite :
But if you lay them on too thick,
    You spoil the matter quite !

" Last, as to the arrangement ;
    Your reader, you should show him,
Must take what information he
    Can get, and look for no im-
mature disclosure of the drift
    And purpose of your poem.

" Therefore, to test his patience—
    How much he can endure—
Mention no places, names, nor dates,
    And evermore be sure
Throughout the poem to be found
    Consistently obscure.

" First fix upon the limit
    To which it shall extend :
Then fill it up with ' padding ',
    (Beg some of any friend) :
Your great *sensation-stanza*
    You place towards the end.

Now try your hand, ere Fancy
    Have lost its present glow——"
" And then," his grandson added,
    " We'll publish it, you know :
Green cloth—gold-lettered at the back,
    In duodecimo ! "
126

Then proudly smiled the old man
  To see the eager lad
Rush madly for his pen and ink
  And for his blotting-pad—
But when he thought of *publishing*,
  His face grew stern and sad.

LEWIS CARROLL.

Ode to the Nightingale

O YOU that from some southern land
  Return with each new spring
To this reviving island and,
  When in the humour, fling
A song so gallant, so divine,
Out on the night, if fairly fine,
As utterly to take the shine
  Out of all birds that sing:

The thrush, grown conscious of your voice,
  Retires behind his leaves,
The blackbird, not at all from choice,
  Sits mopily and grieves;
That wealth of song can e'en transfix
Both dawning owls and farmyard chicks,
And the rude sparrow as he picks
  Things off the couchant beeves.

You are the theme, all themes above,
  The bards have held most dear:
Bar Wordsworth, who preferred the dove,
  Even the most austere
On you have cast their loveliest gems
From Wight to Hampstead or the Thames,
Yet it is one that Fate condemns
  Me ever not to hear.

I have stol'n forth in many a glade
    Where, at their best in June,
Rich nightingales their serenade
    Lift to the solemn moon
So madly that it sometimes stirs
Young wanderers mid the briars and burrs
To sit incautiously on furze,
    Enravished by the tune.

The spinney and the wooded hill,
    The unfrequented lane,
Gardens that throb with song until
    The residents complain,
Though strangers, eager for the sound,
Come trespassing from miles around—
These I have visited, and found
    I always went in vain.

O budded quicks, melodious plots.
    O song so full and free
That livens up those favoured spots
    Often till after three.
O groves so thrilled with high romance
That, though the whole world gaped askance,
I could have sung with half a chance,
    Why are you mute for me?

We cannot all see Grecian urns ;
    Not everywhere one meets
His Lycidas, howe'er he burns
    To emulate those feats ;
But you, immortal bird, art there,
A general theme, with charm to spare,
On which, for all that I'm aware,
    I might have rivalled Keats.

128

But as you please. Unless it's wet,
  When the deep shadows fall
To-night I'll give you one chance yet ;
  If lost, there's no recall.
Sing me your best, and I'll sing you
Something in praise that's really new ;
If you can do without it, do ;
  It's one ode less, that's all.

MAJOR JOHN KENDALL.

XII

NURSERY DAYS

F

F FOR a family taking a walk,
 In Arcadia Terrace, no doubt :
The parents indulge in intelligent talk,
 While the children they gambol about.

At a quarter past six they return to their tea,
 Of a kind that would hardly be tempting to me,
 Though my appetite passes belief.
 There is Jam, Ginger Beer, Buttered Toast, Mar-
 malade,
With a Cold Leg of Mutton and Warm Lemonade,
 And a large Pigeon Pie very skilfully made
 To consist almost wholly of Beef.

Moral.

A Respectable Family taking the air
 Is a subject on which I could dwell ;
It contains all the morals that ever there were,
 And it sets an example as well.

HILAIRE BELLOC.

Obituary

LITTLE Alexander's dead ;
 Jam him in a coffin,
Don't have as good a chance
 For a fun'ral often.
Rush his body right around
 To the cemetery,
Drop him in the sepulchre
 With his Uncle Jerry.

MAX ADELER.

I'M lucky to possess a son
And, what is more, an only one,
Who is (or so it seems to me)
Exactly what a son should be :
In manners, character, physique,
Peerless, a paragon, unique !

I never shall forget my joy
Hearing my firstborn was a boy.
Off to the Club I flew with pride,
To spread .the good news far and wide,
To tell my fellows what I'd done
And how I had achieved a son.

From group to group the tidings flew,
And members whom I scarcely knew
(Or knew too well and couldn't stand)
Came up and shook me by the hand,
Showing a keenness quite intense
To drink my health (at my expense).

And, as they passed the story round,
The Lounge re-echoed with the sound ;
Their sympathetic laughter woke
Our Chairman, old Lord Basingstoke,
Where, full of honours, years, and lunch,
He slumbered, in the throes of *Punch*.

Up in the Card-room, when he heard
The news, poor Colonel Wembley-Byrd
Who'd made a weak " Three Hearts," for fun,
To find that dummy's hand had none,
Threw all his cards upon the floor
And vowed that he would play no more.

134

While, in the so-called Silence Room—
A spot of inspissated gloom—
Two members (well-known clergymen)
Flung down *La Vie Parisienne*
And, with suppressed and tactful mirth,
Discussed the Miracle of Birth.

My oldest friend, Sir Cholmondeley Chubb,
Who was the doyen of the club,
Recalling happier days, long flown,
When he had children of his own,
Described how hard they'd been to bear
And what a perfect curse they were !

And Bishop Bulge, that great divine,
Who always used a little wine
And quoted, as his Pauline plea,
I Timothy v. 23, ·
Toasted my offspring in a quart
Of Pillby's Convalescent Port.

While young Lord Urick Overdraught
(Son of the bankrupt Duke of Graft,
And quite the kindest man alive)
Urged me to lend him two pounds five
Because, as an old friend of ours,
He wished to buy my wife some flow'rs.

You mustn't think that *I'd* forgot
My baby's mother—surely not !
She, too, I knew, had done her bit,
And I appreciated it
And wished she had been there to see
The fuss those fellows made of me.

But when I woke her, late that night,
To tell her, as was only right,
The triumphs I had just enjoyed,
She seemed a little bit annoyed ;
My voice she begged me to subdue,
And not to wake Augustus, too.

Augustus was a sober child ;
For eighteen months he never smiled.
I grew alarmed about his brain,
But specialists who sought in vain
Some reason for this strange affair
Agreed they could find nothing there.

Still I was thankful when, at three,
He grew as bright as bright could be ;
At six he was so sharp and quick,
When shown a dog he'd cry " Tick, tick ! "
When birds across his vision flew
He'd point and say " Bow-wow ! " or " Moo ! "

And when, at ten, he went to school,
To Dr. Pelligrew's (near Poole),
He won respect and love as well
From all who fell beneath his spell ;
They said they'd never met a youth
With such a passion for the truth.

Not once but very many times
When other boys committed crimes
And masters vainly searched about
To try and find the culprit out,
His love of truth compelled my son
To point them out the guilty one.

And so, though never good at games,
He earned those pet endearing names
Which boys confer with ready wit
On any local favourite,
As " Nosey Parker," " Mother's Boy,"
And " Skunk " and " Funk " and " Matron's Joy."

The public school where, later on,
His talents doubtless might have shone,
Proved to be far too rough and rude
For one who with aversion viewed
Those sports in which those fellows got
So very muddy and so hot.

Some people called Augustus fat ;
I wouldn't go so far as that,
For though his figure (which was stout)
Unfitted him to run about,
He could be graceful when he chose,
And quite gazelle-like in repose.

He over-ate at times, perhaps,
And after ev'ry meal would lapse
Into a kind of torpid doze,
Replete and almost comatose,
To wake refreshed and full of zeal
In time for the ensuing meal.

But though the friends who watched him feed
Accused him, now and then, of greed,
And often wished he wouldn't let
His mouth fall open while he ate,
Their criticism he'd disarm ;
They all confessed the boy had charm.

Augustus is at Oxford now,
And though by no means high of brow
He somehow has contrived to get
Into that fashionable set
Whose methods have enhanced the fame
Of Magdalen's once historic name.

His Fair-Isle jumper, I admit,
Though like a glove it seems to fit,
Upon Augustus, only serves
To emphasize those ample curves
Which even his admirers feel
It might be wiser to conceal.

Of course, I know I'm prejudiced,
And yet the bracelets on his wrist,
The jewelled brooch that decks his chest,
Inspire me with a vague unrest ;
I often wish he wouldn't wear
A water-lily in his hair.

And though I feel a deep respect
For those young men of intellect
Who, scorning all the simpler sports,
Don broadbrimmed " bags " (instead of " shorts ")
And read, in a falsetto voice,
The earlier works of Mr. Joyce,

Or verses they themselves have made
Without, it seems, the Muse's aid,
I think the fashion overdone,
And when I see my only son
Beset by all these budding bards,
. . . I wish I'd put him in the Guards !

CAPTAIN HARRY GRAHAM.

A Serenade

" LULLABY, oh, lullaby ! "
Thus I heard a father cry,
" Lullaby, oh, lullaby !
The brat will never shut an eye ;
Hither come, some power divine !
Close his lids, or open mine !

" Lullaby, oh, lullaby !
What the devil makes him cry ?
Lullaby, oh, lullaby !
Still he stares—I wonder why,
Why are not the sons of earth
Blind, like puppies, from the birth ? "

" Lullaby, oh, lullaby ! "
Thus I heard the father cry ;
" Lullaby, oh, lullaby !
Mary, you must come and try !—
Hush, oh, hush, for mercy's sake—
The more I sing, the more you wake ! "

" Lullaby, oh, lullaby !
Fie, you little creature, fie !
Lullaby, oh, lullaby !
Is no poppy-syrup nigh ?
Give him some, or give him all,
I am nodding to his fall ! "

" Lullaby, oh, lullaby !
Two such nights, and I shall die !
Lullaby, oh, lullaby !
He'll be bruised, and so shall I,—
How can I from bedposts keep,
When I'm walking in my sleep ? "

"Lullaby, oh, lullaby!
Sleep his very looks deny—
Lullaby, oh, lullaby;
Nature soon will stupefy—
My nerves relax,—my eyes grow dim—
Who's that fallen—me or him?"

THOMAS HOOD.

The Stern Parent

FATHER heard his children scream,
So he threw them in the stream,
Saying, as he drowned the third,
"Children should be seen, not heard."

CAPTAIN HARRY GRAHAM.

In Memoriam

WILLIE had a purple monkey climbing on a yellow
    stick,
And when he had sucked the paint all off it made
    him deadly sick;
And in his latest hours he clasped that monkey in
    his hand,
And bade good-bye to earth and went into a better
    land.

Oh no more he'll shoot his sister with his little wooden
    gun;
And no more he'll twist the pussy's tail and make
    her yowl for fun.

The pussy's tail now stands out straight ; the gun
    is laid aside ;
The monkey doesn't jump around since little Willie
    died.

MAX ADELER.

Nanny

I SING a long-neglected dame.
Let plays and poets all proclaim
The wonder of the Mother's name,
    And even that of Granny ;
Let others tell with loud hurrahs
The general praises of papas—
I hymn the Mother of Mammas,
    I sing the British Nanny.
Not every pink and girlish thing
    That pushes round a pram,
The ancient rock-like NURSE I sing,
    Britannia's virgin dam,
That, old as mountains and as stout,
From child to child is passed about
Till childless yet, she passes out,
    The lonely British Nanny.

For she it was that from the first
Refused to judge us by our worst ;
We might be yelling fit to burst—
    She crooned a cheerful ditty ;
Our very aunts could not deny
That we were small and ugly fry,
But she with fond prophetic eye
    Maintained that we were pretty.
Alone of all the human race
    She took the kind of view

Of our importance, brain and face,
  That we would have men do ;
And I can never quite forget
No other person I have met
Considered me a perfect pet,
  So here's a health to Nanny !

The artless prattle of a child
Drives everybody nearly wild,
And who that for an hour beguiled
  A babe however clever
For all the riches of the rich
Would undertake a life in which
They lived at that exacting pitch
  Ten hours a day for ever ?
Though even in the mother's joys
  A grander cycle dawns
When we grow more like little boys
  And less like little prawns,
Our Nanny, in a nobler strain,
Would have us at our worst remain,
A babe for ever pink and plain,
  Herself for ever Nanny.

Alas ! the twig becomes a bough ;
We do not need a Nanny now ;
Forgetting her who showed us how,
  We walk to death or glory ;
And whether Fate blows cold or hot,
Whatever women shape our lot,
It's safe to say a Nurse will not
  Be mentioned in the story.
Some other baby far away
  Is hers to soothe or slap.

Some Nelson's in the bath to-day,
　　Some Shelley in her lap ;
And when I think on this small star
How many mighty men there are,
I call for wine and drain a jar
　　To England's noble Nannies.

A. P. HERBERT.

XIII

EXCESS OF PATRIOTISM

A Missouri Maiden's Farewell to Alabama

(A Piece for Recitation)

ALABAMA, good-bye! I love thee well!
But yet for a while do I leave thee now!
Sad, yes, sad thoughts of thee my heart doth swell,
And burning recollections throng my brow!
For I have wandered through thy flowery woods;
Have roamed and read near Tallapoosa's streams,
Have listen'd to Talassee's warring floods,
And woo'd by Coosa's side Aurora's beam.

Yet shame I not to bear an o'er-full heart,
Nor blush to turn behind my tearful eyes,
'Tis from no stranger land I now must part,
'Tis to no strangers left I yield these sighs.
Welcome and home were mine within this State,
Whose vales I leave, whose spires fade fast from me
And cold must be mine eyes and heart and tête,
Ere, dear Alabama! They turn cold on thee!

MARK TWAIN.

England

(A Sonnet by Mr. Mayhem in "Caliban's Guide to Learning")

ENGLAND, if ever it should be thy fate
  By fortune's turn or accident of chance
To fall from craven fears of being great,
  And in the tourney with dishevelled lance
To topple headlong, and incur the Hate
  Of Spain, America, Germany, and France,
What will you find upon that dreadful date
  To check the backward move of your advance?

147

A little Glory ; purchased not with gold
    Nor yet with Frankincense (the island blood
Is incommensurate, neither bought nor sold),
    But on the poop where Drake and Nelson stood
An iron hand, a stern unflinching eye
To meet the large assaults of Destiny.

HILAIRE BELLOC.

XIV

STORIES OF LAND AND SEA

The Bumboat Woman's Story

I'M old, my dears, and shrivelled with age, and work,
  and grief,
My eyes are gone, and my teeth have been drawn
  by Time, the Thief!
For terrible sights I've seen, and dangers great I've
  run—
I'm nearly seventy now, and my work is almost
  done!

Ah! I've been young in my time, and I've played the
  deuce with men!
I'm speaking of ten years past—I was barely sixty
  then:
My cheeks were mellow and soft, and my eyes were
  large and sweet,
POLL PINEAPPLE'S eyes were the standing toast of
  the Royal Fleet!

A bumboat woman was I, and I faithfully served the
  ships
With apples and cakes, and fowls and beer, and halfpenny dips,
And beef for the generous mess, where the officers
  dine at nights,
And fine fresh peppermint drops for the rollicking
  midshipmites.

Of all the kind commanders who anchored in Ports-
  mouth Bay,
By far the sweetest of all was kind LIEUTENANT
  BELAYE.

Lieutenant Belaye commanded the gunboat *Hot
Cross Bun,*
She was seven and seventy feet in length, and she
carried a gun.

With the laudable view of enhancing his country's
naval pride,
When people inquired her size, Lieutenant Belaye
replied,
" Oh, my ship, my ship is the first of the Hundred
and Twenty-ones ! "
Which meant her tonnage, but people imagined it
meant her guns.

Whenever I went on board he would beckon me down
below,
" Come down, Little Buttercup, come " (for he loved
to call me so),
And he'd tell of the fights at sea in which he'd taken
a part,
And so Lieutenant Belaye won poor Poll Pineapple's heart !

But at length his orders came, and he said one day,
said he,
" I'm ordered to sail with the *Hot Cross Bun* to the
German Sea."
And the Portsmouth maidens wept when they learnt
the evil day,
For every Portsmouth maid loved good Lieutenant
Belaye.

And I went to a back back street, with plenty of
cheap cheap shops,
And I bought an oilskin hat, and a second-hand suit
of slops,

And I went to LIEUTENANT BELAYE (and he never
   suspected *me* !)
And I entered myself as a chap as wanted to go to
   sea.

We sailed that afternoon at the mystic hour of one,—
Remarkably nice young men were the crew of the
   Hot Cross Bun.
I'm sorry to say that I've heard that sailors some-
   times swear,
But I never yet heard a *Bun* say anything wrong, I
   declare.

When Jack Tars meet, they meet with a " Messmate,
   ho ! What cheer ? "
But here, on the *Hot Cross Bun*, it was " How do you
   do, my dear ? "
When Jack Tars growl, I believe they growl with a
   big big D—
But the strongest oath of the *Hot Cross Bun* was a
   mild " Dear me ! "

Yet, though they were all well bred, you could
   scarcely call them slick :
Whenever a sea was on, they were all extremely
   sick ;
And whenever the weather was calm, and the wind
   was light and fair,
They spent more time than a sailor should on his
   back back hair.

They certainly shivered and shook when ordered
   aloft to run,
And they screamed when LIEUTENANT BELAYE dis-
   charged his only gun.

153

And as he was proud of his gun—such pride is hardly
  wrong—
The Lieutenant was blazing away at intervals all
  day long.

They all agreed very well, though at times you heard
  it said
That BILL had a way of his own of making his lips
  look red—
That JOE looked quite his age—or somebody might
  declare
That BARNACLE'S long pig-tail was never his own
  own hair.

BELAYE would admit that his men were of no great
  use to him,
" But then," he would say, " there is little to do on
  a gun-boat trim.
I can hand, and reef, and steer, and fire my big gun
  too—
And it *is* such a treat to sail with a gentle well-bred
  crew."

I saw him every day ! How the happy moments
  sped !
Reef topsails ! Make all taut ! There s dirty weather
  ahead !
(I do not mean that tempests threatened the *Hot
  Cross Bun* :
In *that* case, I don't know whatever we *should* have
  done !)

After a fortnight's cruise we put into port one day,
And off on leave for a week went kind LIEUTENANT
  BELAYE,

And after a long long week had passed (and it seemed
    like a life),
LIEUTENANT BELAYE returned to his ship with a fair
    young wife !

He up, and he says, says he, " Oh, crew of the *Hot
    Cross Bun*,
Here is the wife of my heart, for the Church has
    made us one ! "
And as he uttered the word, the crew went out of
    their wits,
And all fell down in so many separate fainting fits.

And then their hair came down, or off, as the case
    might be,
And lo ! the rest of the crew were simple girls, like
    me,
Who all had fled from their homes in a sailor's blue
    array,
To follow the shifting fate of kind LIEUTENANT
    BELAYE !

It's strange to think that *I* should ever have loved
    young men,
But I'm speaking of ten years past—I was barely
    sixty then ;
And now my cheeks are furrowed with grief and age,
    I trow !
And poor POLL PINEAPPLE'S eyes have lost their
    lustre now !

SIR W. S. GILBERT.

Burglar Bill

THROUGH a window in the attic
    Brawny Burglar Bill has crept ;
Seeking stealthily the wardrobe
    Where the jewellery is kept.

He is furnished with a " jemmy,"
    Centre-bit, and carpet-bag,
For the latter " comes in handy,"
    So he says, " to stow the swag."

Here, upon the second landing,
    He, secure, may work his will :
Down below's a dinner-party,
    Up above—the house is still.

Suddenly—in spell-bound horror,
    All his satisfaction ends—
For a little white-robed figure
    By the banister descends !

Bill has reached for his revolver,
    Yet—he hesitates to fire. . . .
Child is it ? or—apparition,
    That provokes him to perspire ?

Can it be his guardian angel,
    Sent to stay his hand from crime ?
He could wish she had selected,
    Some more seasonable time !

" Go away ! " he whispers hoarsely,
    " Burglars hev their bread to earn.
I don't need no Gordian angel
    Givin' of me sech a *turn* ! "

But the blue eyes open wider,
    Ruby lips reveal their pearl ;
" I is not a Garden anzel,
    Only—dust a yickle dirl !

" On the thtairs to thit I'm doin'
    Till the tarts and dellies tum ;
Partinthon (our butler) alwayth
    Thaves for Baby Bella thome !

" Poor man, 'oo is yookin' 'ungwy—
    Leave 'oo burgling fings up dere ;
Tum viz me and share the sweeties,
    Thitting on the bottom thtair ! "

" Reely, Miss, you must excoose me ! "
    Says the Burglar with a jerk :
" Dooty calls, and time is pressing ;
    I must set about my work ! "

" Is 'oo work to bweak in houses ?
    Nana *told* me so, I'm sure !
Will 'oo twy if 'oo can manage
    To bweak in my *dolls'-house* door ?

" I tan *never* det it undone,
    So my dollies tan't det out ;
They don't *yike* the fwont to open
    Every time they'd walk about !

" Twy, and—if 'oo does it nithely—
    When I'm thent upthtairs to thleep,
I will bwing 'oo up thome doodies,
    'Oo shall have them all—to keep ! "

Off the little " angel " flutters ;
    But the burglar—mops his brow.
He is wholly unaccustomed
    To a kindly greeting now !

Never with a smile of welcome
    Has he seen his entrance met !
Nobody—except the policeman—
    Ever wanted *him* as yet !

Many a stately home he's entered,
    But, with unobtrusive tact,
He has ne'er, in paying visits,
    Called attention to the fact.

Gain he counts it, on departing,
    Should he have avoided strife.
Ah, my brothers, but the Burglar's
    Is a sad, a lonely life !

All forgotten now the jewels,
    Once the purpose of his " job " ;
Down he sinks upon the door-mat,
    With a deep and choking sob.

Then, the infant's plea recalling,
    Seeks the nursery above ;
Looking for the Lilliputian
    Crib he is to crack—for *love* !

In the corner stands the Dolls'-house,
  Gaily painted green and red ;
And its door declines to open,
  Even as the child has said !

Forth came centre-bit and jemmy :
  All his implements are plied ;
Never has he burgled better !
  As he feels, with honest pride.

Deftly is the task accomplished,
  For the door will open well ;
When—a childish voice behind him
  Breaks the silence like a bell.

" Sank'oo, Misser Burglar, sank 'oo !
  And, betause 'oo's been so nice,
See what I have dot—a cheesecake !
  Gweat big gweedies ate the ice."

" Papa says he wants to see 'oo,
  Partinthon is tummin too—
Tan't 'oo wait ? "
                  " Well, *not* this evenin',
  So, my little dear,—a doo ! "

Fast he speeds across the housetops !—
  But his bosom throbs with bliss
For upon his rough lips linger
  Traces of a baby's kiss.

Dreamily on downy pillow
  Baby Bella murmurs sweet :
" Burglar—tum adain, and thee me . . .
  I will dive 'oo cakes to eat ! "

In a garret, worn, and weary,
   Burglar Bill has sunk to rest,
Clasping tenderly a crumpled
   Cheesecake to his burly breast.

F. ANSTEY.

Plain Language from Truthful James

WHICH I wish to remark,
   And my language is plain,
That for ways that are dark
   And for tricks that are vain,
The heathen Chinee is peculiar,
   Which the same I would rise to explain.

Ah Sin was his name ;
   And I shall not deny,
In regard to the same,
   What that name might imply ;
But his smile it was pensive and child-like,
   As I frequent remarked to Bill Nye.

It was August the third,
   And quite soft was the skies ;
Which it might be inferred
   That Ah Sin was likewise ;
Yet he played it that day upon William
   And me in a way I despise.

Which we had a small game,
   And Ah Sin took a hand :
It was euchre. The same
   He did not understand ;
But he smiled as he sat by the table,
   With the smile that was child-like and bland.
160

Yet the cards they were stocked
    In a way that I grieve,
And my feelings were shocked
    By the state of Nye's sleeve,
Which was stuffed full of aces and bowers,
    And the same with intent to deceive.

But the hands that were played
    By that heathen Chinee,
And the points that he made,
    Were quite frightful to see,—
Till at last he put down a right bower,
    Which the same Nye had dealt unto me.

Then I looked upon Nye,
    And he gazed upon me ;
And he rose with a sigh,
    And said, " Can this be ?
We are ruined with Chinese cheap labour,"—
    And he went for that heathen Chinee.

In the scene that ensued
    I did not take a hand,
But the floor it was strewed
    Like the leaves on the strand
With the cards that Ah Sin had been hiding,
    In the game he " did not understand."

In his sleeves, which were long,
    He had twenty-four packs,—
Which was coming it strong,
    Yet I state but the facts ;
And we found on his nails, which were taper,
    What is frequent in tapers,—that's wax.

Which is why I remark,
    And my language is plain,
That for ways that are dark
    And for tricks that are vain,
The heathen Chinee is peculiar,—
    Which the same I am free to maintain.

BRET HARTE.

The Aged Pilot Man

On the Erie Canal it was,
    All on a summer's day,
I sailed forth with my parents
    Far away to Albany.

From out the clouds at noon that day
    There came a dreadful storm,
That piled the billows high about
    And filled us with alarm.

A man came rushing from a house,
    Saying, "Snub up [1] your boat, I pray !
Snub up your boat, snub up, alas !
    Snub up while yet you may."

Our captain cast one glance astern,
    Then forward glancèd he,
And said, "My wife and little ones
    I never more shall see."

Said Dollinger, the pilot man,
    In noble words, but few,—
"Fear not, but lean on Dollinger,
    And he will fetch you through."

[1] The customary canal technicality for "tie up."

162

The boat drove on, the frightened mules
   Tore through the rain and wind,
And bravely still, in danger's post,
   The whip-boy strode behind.

" Come 'board, come 'board," the captain cried,
   " Nor tempt so wild a storm " ;
But still the raging mules advanced,
   And still the boy strode on.

Then said the captain to us all,
   " Alas, 'tis plain to me,
The greater danger is not there,
   But here upon the sea.

" So let us strive, while life remains,
   To save all souls on board,
And then if die at last we must,
   Let . . . I *cannot* speak the word ! "

Said Dollinger, the pilot man,
   Tow'ring above the crew,
" Fear not, but trust in Dollinger,
   And he will fetch you through."

" Low bridge ! low bridge ! " all heads went down,
   The labouring bark went on ;
A mill we passed, we passed a church,
   Hamlets, and fields of corn,
And all the world came out to see,
   And chased along the shore,

Crying, " Alas, alas, the sheeted rain,
   The wind, the tempest's roar !
Alas, the gallant ship and crew,
   Can *nothing* help them more ? "

And from our deck sad eyes looked out
   Across the stormy scene :
The tossing wake of billows aft,
   The bending forests green,

The chickens sheltered under carts,
   In lee of barn the cows,
The skurrying swine with straw in mouth,
   The wild spray from our bows !

        " She balances !
        She wavers !
Now let her go about !
   If she misses stays and broaches to,
We're all "—[then with a shout,]
        " Hurray ! hurray !
        Avast ! belay !
        Take in more sail !
        Lord, what a gale !
Ho, boy, haul taut on the hind **mule's tail** ! "

" Ho ! lighten ship ! ho ! man the pump !
Ho, hostler, heave the lead !
" A quarter-three !—'tis shoaling fast !
Three feet large !—t-h-r-e-e feet !—
Three feet scant ! " I cried in fright,
   " Oh, is there *no* retreat ? "

Said Dollinger, the pilot man,
   As on the vessel flew,
" Fear not, but trust in Dollinger,
   And he will fetch you through."

A panic struck the bravest hearts,
   The boldest cheek grew pale ;
164

For plain to all, this shoaling said
A leak had burst the ditch's bed !
And straight as bolt from crossbow sped,
Our ship swept on, with shoaling lead,
  Before the fearful gale !

" Sever the tow-line ! Cripple the mules ! "
  Too late ! . . . There comes a shock !
       *   *   *
Another length, and the fated craft
  Would have swum in the saving lock !

Then gathered together the shipwrecked crew
  And took one last embrace,
While sorrowful tears from despairing eyes
  Ran down each hopeless face ;

And some did think of their little ones
  Whom they never more might see,
And others of waiting wives at home,
  And mothers that grieved would be.

But of all the children of misery there
  On that poor sinking frame,
But one spake words of hope and faith,
  And I worshipped as they came :
Said Dollinger, the pilot man,—
  (O brave heart, strong, and true !)—
  " Fear not, but trust in Dollinger,
  For he will fetch you through."

Lo ! scarce the words have passed his lips,
  The dauntless prophet say'th,
When every soul about him seeth
  A wonder crown his faith !

" And count ye all, both great and small,
  As numbered with the dead!
For mariner for forty year,
  On Erie, boy and man,
I never yet saw such a storm,
  Or one't with it began! "

So overboard a keg of nails
  And anvils three we threw,
Likewise four bales of gunny-sacks,
  Two hundred pounds of glue,
Two sacks of corn, four ditto wheat,
  A box of books, a cow,
A violin, Lord Byron's works,
  A rip-saw and a sow.

A curve! a curve! the dangers grow!
" Labbord! — stabbord! — s-t-e-a-d-y! — so!—
Hard-a-port, Dol!—hellum-a-lee!
Haw the head mule!—the aft one gee!
Luff!—bring her to the wind! "

For straight a farmer brought a plank—
  (Mysteriously inspired),—
And laying it unto the ship,
  In silent awe retired.

Then every sufferer stood amazed
  That pilot man before;
A moment stood; then wondering turned,
  And speechless walked ashore.

MARK TWAIN.

166

You may lift me up in your arms, lad, and turn my
    face to the sun,
For a last look back at the dear old track where the
    Jubilee Cup was won ;
And draw your chair to my side, lad—no, thank ye,
    I feel no pain—
For I'm going out with the tide, lad, but I'll tell you
    the tale again.

I'm seventy-nine or nearly, and my head it has long
    turned grey,
But it all comes back as clearly as though it was
    yesterday—
The dust, and the bookies shouting around the clerk
    of the scales,
And the clerk of the course, and the nobs in force,
    and 'Is 'Ighness the Pr**ce of W*les.

'Twas a nine-hole thresh to wind'ard (but non eof
    us cared for that),
With a straight run home to the service tee, and a
    finish along the flat,
" Stiff ? " ah, well you may say it ! Spot barred,
    and at five stone ten !
But at two and a bisque I'd ha' run the risk ; for I
    was a greenhorn then.

So we stripped to the B. Race signal, the old red
    swallowtail—
There was young Ben Bolt and the Portland Colt,
    and Aston Villa, and Yale ;
And W.G., and Steinitz, Leander and The Saint,
And the G*rm*n Emp*r*r's Meteor, a-looking as
    fresh as paint ;

John Roberts (scratch), and Safety Match, The
Lascar, and Lorna Doone,
Oom Paul (a bye), and Romany Rye, and me upon
Wooden Spoon ;
And some of us cut for partners, and some of us
strung for baulk,
And some of us tossed for stations—But there, what
use to talk ?

Three-quarter-back on the Kingsclere crack was
station enough for me,
With a fresh jackyarder blowing and the Vicarage
goal a-lee !
And I leaned and patted her centre-bit, and eased
the quid in her cheek,
With a " Soh my lass ! " and a " Woa you brute ! "
—for she could do all but speak.

She was geared a thought too high perhaps ; she
was trained a trifle fine ;
But she had the grand reach forward ! I never saw
such a line !
Smooth-bored, clean run, from her fiddle head with
its dainty ear half-cock,
Hard-bit, *pur sang*, from her overhang to the heel of
her off hind sock.

Sir Robert he walked beside me as I worked her
down to the mark ;
" There's money on this, my lad," said he, " and
most of 'em's running dark ;
But ease this sheet if you're bunkered, and pack
the scrummages tight,
And use your slide at the distance, and we'll drink
to your health to-night ! "

But I bent and tightened my stretcher. Said I to
     myself, said I—
" John Jones, this here is the Jubilee Cup, and you
     have to do or die."
And the words weren't hardly spoken when the
     umpire shouted " Play ! "
And we all kicked off from the Gasworks End with
     a " Yoicks ! " and a " Gone Away ! "

And at first I thought of nothing, as the clay flew
     by in lumps,
But stuck to the old Ruy Lopez, and wondered
     who'd call for trumps,
And luffed her close to the cushion, and watched
     each one as it broke,
And in triple file up the Rowley Mile we went like
     a trail of smoke.

The Lascar made the running but he didn't amount
     to much,
For old Oom Paul was quick on the ball, and headed
     it back to touch ;
And the whole first flight led off with the right as
     The Saint took up the pace,
And drove it clean to the putting green and trumped
     it there with an ace.

John Roberts had given a miss in baulk, but Villa
     cleared with a punt ;
And keeping her service hard and low the Meteor
     forged to the front ;
With Romany Rye to windward at dormy and two
     to play,
And Yale close up—but a Jubilee Cup isn't run for
     every day.

We laid our course for the Warner—I tell you the
pace was hot !
And again off Tattenham Corner a blanket covered
the lot.
Check side ! Check side ! now steer her wide ! and
barely an inch of room,
With The Lascar's tail over our lee rail and brushing
Leander's boom.

We were running as strong as ever—eight knots—
but it couldn't last ;
For the spray and the bails were flying, the whole
field tailing fast ;
And the Portland Colt had shot his bolt, and Yale
was bumped at the Doves,
And The Lascar resigned to Steinitz, stalemated in
fifteen moves.

It was bellows to mend with Roberts—starred three
for a penalty kick :
But he chalked his cue and gave 'em the butt, and
Oom Paul marked the trick—
" Offside—No Ball—and at fourteen all ! Mark
Cock ! and two for his nob ! "
When W.G. ran clean through his lee and beat him
twice with a lob.

He yorked him twice on a crumbling pitch and wiped
his eye with a brace,
But his guy-rope split with the strain of it and he
dropped back out of the race ;
And I drew a bead on the Meteor's lead, and chal-
lenging none too soon,
Bent over and patted her garboard strake, and called
upon Wooden Spoon.

She was all of a shiver forward, the spoondrift thick
    on her flanks,
But I'd brought her an easy gambit, and nursed her
    over the banks ;
She answered her helm—the darling ! and woke up
    now with a rush,
While the Meteor's jock, he sat like a rock—he knew
    we rode for his brush !

There was no one else left in it. The Saint was using
    his whip,
And Safety Match with a lofting catch, was pocketed
    deep at slip ;
And young Ben Bolt with his niblick took miss at
    Leander's lunge,
But topped the net with the ricochet, and Steinitz
    threw up the sponge.

But none of the lot could stop the rot—nay, don't
    ask *me* to stop !
The Villa had called for lemons, Oom Paul had taken
    his drop,
And both were kicking the referee. Poor fellow !
    he done his best ;
But, being in doubt, he'd ruled them out—which
    he always did when pressed.

So, inch by inch, I tightened the winch, and chucked
    the sandbags out—
I heard the nursery cannons pop, I heard the bookies
    shout :
" The Meteor wins ! " " No, Wooden Spoon ! "
    " Check ! " " Vantage ! " " Leg Before ! "
" Last Lap ! " " Pass Nap ! " At his saddle-flap
    I put up the helm and wore.

You may overlap at the saddle-flap, and yet be
    loo'd on the tape :
And it all depends upon changing ends, how a seven-
    year-old will shape ;
It was tack and tack to the Lepe and back—a fair
    ding-dong to the Ridge,
And he led by his forward canvas yet as we shot
    'neath Hammersmith Bridge.

He led by his forward canvas—he led from his
    strongest suit—
But along we went on a roaring scent, and at Fawley
    I gained a foot.
He fisted off with his jigger, and gave me his wash—
    too late !
Deuce—Vantage—Check ! By neck and neck we
    rounded into the straight.

I could hear the " Conquering 'Ero " a-crashing on
    Godfrey's band,
And my hopes fell sudden to zero, just there, with
    the race in hand—
In sight of the Turf's Blue Ribbon, in sight of the
    umpire's tape,
As I felt the tack of her spinnaker c-rack ! as I heard
    the steam escape !

Had I lost at that awful juncture my presence of
    mind ? . . . but no !
I leaned and felt for the puncture, and plugged it
    there with my toe . . .
Hand over hand by the Members' Stand I lifted and
    eased her up,
Shot—clean and fair—to the crossbar there, and
    landed the Jubilee Cup !

" The odd by a head, and leg before," so the Judge
    he gave the word :
And the Umpire shouted " Over ! " but I neither
    spoke nor stirred.
They crowded round : for there on the ground I
    lay in a dead-cold swoon,
Pitched neck and crop on the turf atop of my beauti-
    ful Wooden Spoon.

Her dewlap tire was punctured, her bearings all red
    hot ;
She'd a lolling tongue, and her bowsprit sprung, and
    her running gear in a knot ;
And amid the sobs of her backers, Sir Robert
    loosened her girth
And led her away to the knacker's. She had raced
    her last on earth !

But I mind me well of the tear that fell from the eye
    of our noble Pr*nce,
And the things he said as he tucked me in bed—and
    I've lain there ever since ;
Tho' it all gets mixed up queerly that happened
    before my spill,—
But I draw my thousand yearly : it'll pay for the
    doctor's bill.

I'm going out with the tide, lad—you'll dig me a
    numble grave,
And whiles you will bring your bride, lad, and your
    sons, if sons you have,
And there when the dews are weeping, and the echoes
    murmur " Peace ! "
And the salt, salt tide comes creeping and covers
    the popping-crease ;

N

In the hour when the ducks deposit their eggs with
    a boasted force,
They'll look and whisper " How was it ? " and you'll
    take them over the course,
And your voice will break as you try to speak of the
    glorious first of June,
When the Jubilee Cup, with John Jones up, was won
    upon Wooden Spoon.

SIR A. QUILLER-COUCH.

The Duel

A Serious Ballad

" Like the two Kings of Brentford smelling at one
nosegay."

In Brentford town, of old renown,
    There lived a Mister Bray,
Who fell in love with Lucy Bell,
    And so did Mr. Clay.

To see her ride from Hammersmith,
    By all it was allowed,
Such fair outsides are seldom seen,
    Such Angels on a Cloud.

Said Mr. Bray to Mr. Clay,
    You choose to rival me,
And court Miss Bell, but there your court
    No thoroughfare shall be.

Unless you now give up your suit,
    You may repent your love ;
I who have shot a pigeon match,
    Can shoot a turtle dove.

174

So pray before you woo her more,
  Consider what you do ;
If you pop aught to Lucy Bell—
  I'll pop it into you.

Said Mr. Clay to Mr. Bray,
  Your threats I quite explode ;
One who has been a volunteer
  Knows how to prime and load.

And so I say to you unless
  Your passion quiet keeps,
I who have shot and hit bulls' eyes,
  May chance to hit a sheep's.

Now gold is oft for silver changed,
  And that for copper red ;
But these two went away to give
  Each other change for lead.

But first they sought a friend apiece,
  This pleasant thought to give—
When they were dead, they thus should have
  Two seconds still to live.

To measure out the ground not long
  The seconds then forbore,
And having taken one rash step,
  They took a dozen more.

They next prepared each pistol-pan
  Against the deadly strife,
By putting in the prime of death
  Against the prime of life.

Now all was ready for the foes,
  But when they took their stands,
Fear made them tremble so, they found
  They both were shaking hands.

Said Mr. C. to Mr. B.,
  Here one of us may fall,
And like St. Paul's Cathedral now
  Be doomed to have a ball.

I do confess I did attach
  Misconduct to your name ;
If I withdraw the charge, will then
  Your ramrod do the same ?

Said Mr. B., I do agree—
  But think of Honour's Courts !
If we go off without a shot,
  There will be strange reports.

But look, the morning now is bright,
  Though cloudy it begun :
Why can't we aim above, as if
  We had called out the sun ?

So up into the harmless air
  Their bullets they did send ;
And may all other duels have
  That upshot in the end !

THOMAS HOOD.

Faithless Sally Brown

An Old Ballad

YOUNG Ben he was a nice young man,
 A carpenter by trade ;
And he fell in love with Sally Brown,
 That was a lady's maid.

But as they fetch'd a walk one day,
 They met a press-gang crew ;
And Sally she did faint away,
 Whilst Ben he was brought to.

The Boatswain swore with wicked words,
 Enough to shock a saint,
But though she did seem in a fit,
 'Twas nothing but a feint.

" Come, girl," said he, " hold up your head,
 He'll be as good as me ;
For when your swain is in our boat,
 A boatswain he will be."

So when they'd made their game of her,
 And taken off her elf,
She roused, and found she only was
 A-coming to herself.

" And is he gone, and is he gone ? "
 She cried, and wept outright :
" Then I will to the water-side
 And see him out of sight."

A waterman came up to her,—
"Now, young woman," said he,
"If you weep on so, you will make
Eye-water in the sea."

"Alas! they've taken my beau, Ben,
To sail with old Benbow";
And her woe began to run afresh,
As if she'd said Gee woe!

Says he, "They've only taken him
To the Tender-ship, you see";—
"The Tender-ship," cried Sally Brown,
"What a hard-ship that must be!

"O! would I were a mermaid now,
For then I'd follow him;
But, oh! I'm not a fish-woman,
And so I cannot swim.

"Alas! I was not born beneath
'The virgin and the scales,'
So I must curse my cruel stars,
And walk about in Wales."

Now Ben had sail'd to many a place
That's underneath the world;
But in two years the ship came home,
And all the sails were furl'd.

But when he call'd on Sally Brown,
To see how she went on,
He found she'd got another Ben,
Whose Christian name was John.

" O Sally Brown, O Sally Brown,
  How could you serve me so,
I've met with many a breeze before,
  But never such a blow ! "

Then reading on his 'bacco box,
  He heaved a heavy sigh,
And then began to eye his pipe,
  And then to pipe his eye.

And then he tried to sing " All's Well,"
  But could not, though he tried ;
His head was turn'd, and so he chew'd
  His pigtail till he died.

His death, which happen'd in his berth,
  At forty-odd befell :
They went and told the sexton, and
  The sexton toll'd the bell.

                              THOMAS HOOD.

Peter the Wag

POLICEMAN PETER FORTH I drag
  From his obscure retreat :
He was a merry, genial wag,
  Who loved a mad conceit.
If he were asked the time of day
  By country bumpkins green,
He not unfrequently would say
  " A quarter past thirteen."

If ever you by word of mouth
  Inquired of Mr. Forth
The way to somewhere in the South
  He always sent you North.

With little boys his beat along
  He loved to stop and play;
He loved to send old ladies wrong
  And teach their feet to stray.

He would in frolic moments, when
  Such mischief bent upon,
Take Bishops up as betting men,
  Bid Ministers move on.
Then all the worthy boys he knew
  He regularly licked,
And always collared people who
  Had had their pockets picked.

He was not naturally bad,
  Or viciously inclined,
But from his early youth he had
  A waggish turn of mind.
The Men of London grimly scowled
  With indignation wild:
The Men of London gruffly growled,
  But Peter calmly smiled.

Against this minion of the Crown
  The swelling murmurs grew—
From Camberwell to Kentish Town—
  From Rotherhithe to Kew.
Still humoured he his wagsome turn,
  And fed in various ways
The coward rage that dared to burn
  But did not dare to blaze.

Still, Retribution has her day
  Although her flight is slow:
One day that Crusher lost his way
  Near Poland Street, Soho.

The haughty youth, too proud to ask,
  To find his way resolved,
And in the tangle of his task
  Got more and more involved.

The Men of London, overjoyed,
  Came there to jeer their foe—
And flocking crowds completely cloyed
  The mazes of Soho ;
The news, on telegraphic wires,
  Sped swiftly o'er the lea—
Excursions from distant shires
  Brought myriads to see.

For weeks he trod his self-made beats
  Through Newport, Gerrard, Bear,
Greek, Rupert, Frith, Dean, Poland Streets,
  And into Golden Square :
But all alas, in vain, for when
  He tried to learn the way
Of little boys or grown-up men
  They none of them would say.

Their eyes would flash—their teeth would grind—
  Their lips would tightly curl—
They'd say, " Thy way thyself must find,
  Thou misdirecting churl ! "
And similarly, also, when
  He tried a foreign friend ;
Italians answered, " Il balen "—
  The French, " No comprehend."

The Russ would say with gleaming eye
  " Sevastopol ! " and groan.
The Greek said " Tupto, tuptomai,
  Tupto, tuptein, tupton."

To wander thus for many a year
　　That Crusher never ceased—
The Men of London dropped a tear,
　　Their anger was appeased.

At length exploring gangs were sent
　　To find poor Forth's remains—
A handsome grant by Parliament
　　Was voted for their pains.
To seek the poor policeman out
　　Bold spirits volunteered,
And when at last they solved the doubt
　　The Men of London cheered.

And in a yard, dark, dank, and drear,
　　They found him, on the floor—
(It leads from Richmond Buildings—near
　　The Royalty stage door.)
With brandy cold and brandy hot
　　They plied him, starved and wet,
And made him sergeant on the spot—
　　The Men of London's pet !

SIR. W. S. GILBERT.

The Society upon the Stanislaus

I reside at Table Mountain, and my name is Truth-
　　ful James ;
I am not up to small deceit or any sinful games ;
And I'll tell in simple language what I know about
　　the row
That broke up our Society upon the Stanislow.

182

But first I would remark, that it is not a proper
     plan
For any scientific gent to whale his fellow-man,
And if a member don't agree with his peculiar whim,
To lay for that same member for to " put a head "
     on him.

Now nothing could be finer or more beautiful to see
Than the first six months' proceedings of that same
     Society,
Till Brown of Calaveras brought a lot of fossil bones
That he found within a tunnel near the tenement of
     Jones.

Then Brown he read a paper, and he reconstructed
     there,
From those same bones, an animal that was extremely
     rare ;
And Jones then asked the Chair for a suspension of
     the rules,
Till he could prove that those same bones was one
     of his lost mules.

Then Brown he smiled a bitter smile, and said he was
     at fault,
It seemed he had been trespassing on Jones's family
     vault ;
He was a most sarcastic man, this quiet Mr. Brown,
And on several occasions he had cleaned out the
     town.

Now I hold it is not decent for a scientific gent
To say another is an ass,—at least, to all intent ;
Nor should the individual who happens to be meant
Reply by heaving rocks at him, to any great extent.

183

Then Abner Dean of Angel's raised a point of order,
when
A chunk of old red sandstone took him in the abdo-
men,
And he smiled a kind of sickly smile, and curled up
on the floor,
And the subsequent proceedings interested him no
more.

For, in less time than I write it, every member did
engage
In a warfare with the remnants of a palæozoic age ;
And the way théy heaved those fossils in their anger
was a sin,
Till the skull of an old mammoth caved the head of
Thompson in.

And this is all I have to say of these improper games,
For I live at Table Mountain, and my name in Truth-
ful James ;
And I've told in simple language what I knew about
the row
That broke up our Society upon the Stanislow.

                                        BRET HARTE.

XV

DOGS

Epigram

Engraved on the collar of a dog which I gave to His Royal Highness

I AM his Highness' dog at Kew ;
Pray tell me, sir, whose dog are you ?

POPE.

The Poodle and the Pug

WHEN I was a High School noodle
  And life was rather smug,
My father kept a poodle
  My mother kept a pug,
And every Sunday, after three,
This strange procession you might see,
My dear Papa, Mamma and me,
  The poodle and the pug.

The poodle I could never bear,
For he was naked here and there
And, partly bare and partly hair,
  Was like a worn-out rug ;
The pug, upon the other hand,
Was far too well upholstered, and
Somehow the pug I could not stand,
  I could not stand the pug.
Oh dear, how I disliked those dogs,
The pug had features like a frog's,
And deep in the profoundest bogs
  Could I have put that pug.

187

For every Sunday, after three,
This strange procession you might see,
My dear Papa, Mamma and me,
    The poodle and the pug.

The poodle was alert and gay,
He liked to run in front and play
In quite a Continental way,
    Unlike the pompous pug ;
The pug was the more Saxon kind,
He plodded on a mile behind
And in his movements called to mind
    An alderman, or slug.
And that explains the life I led,
For it was I who, rather red,
Pursued the poodle far ahead,
    Or waited for the pug.

And every Sunday, after three,
This strange procession you might see,
My dear Papa, Mamma and me,
    The poodle and the pug.

These dogs have left their mark on me ;
So many citizens I see
A sort of poodle seem to be,
    Or else a sort of pug.
At ballets of the Russian kind
Whole packs of poodles you will find,
With tufts of hair stuck here and there,
    Which one would like to tug ;
While as for pugs, if you reflect,
You know a dozen, I expect ;
Well, Mrs. Bun at Number One,
    Is definitely pug.

And you, when you go beddy-bye,
Look in your mirror, eye to eye,
And put the question, " Which am I ?
   A poodle or a pug ? "

I cannot tell upon what grounds
I sing of these unpleasant hounds ;
The Muse proceeds by leaps and bounds,
   One follows with a shrug ;
But this is what occurs to me :—
Degraded though the age may be,
At any rate we seldom see
   A poodle or a pug ;
Our ways would make our fathers weep,
Our skirts too short, our drinks too deep,
But dash it all, we do *not* keep
   A poodle or a pug !

And you, my child, will never be
Compelled on Sundays, after three,
To walk with your Mamma and me,
   A poodle and a pug.

A. P. HERBERT.

Elegy on the Death of a Mad Dog

GOOD people all, of every sort,
   Give ear unto my song,
And if you find it wondrous short—
   It cannot hold you long.

In Islington there was a man,
   Of whom the world might say,
That still a godly race he ran—
   Whene'er he went to pray.

A kind and gentle heart he had,
    To comfort friends and foes ;
The naked every day he clad—
    When he put on his clothes.

And in that town a dog was found,
    As many dogs there be,
Both mongrel, puppy, whelp, and hound,
    And curs of low degree.

This dog and man at first were friends ;
    But when a pique began,
The dog, to gain some private ends,
    Went mad, and bit the man.

Around from all the neighbouring streets
    The wondering neighbours ran,
And swore the dog had lost its wits,
    To bite so good a man.

The wound it seem'd both sore and sad,
    To every Christian eye ;
And while they swore the dog was mad,
    They swore the man would die.

But soon a wonder came to light,
    That show'd the rogues they lied ;
The man recover'd of the bite—
    The dog it was that died.

                              OLIVER GOLDSMITH.

On a Spaniel called "Beau" killing a Young Bird

A SPANIEL, Beau, that fares like you,
  Well-fed, and at his ease,
Should wiser be than to pursue
  Each trifle that he sees.

But you have killed a tiny bird,
  Which flew not till to-day,
Against my orders, whom you heard
  Forbidding you the prey.

My dog! what remedy remains,
  Since, teach you all I can,
I see you, after all my pains,
  So much resemble man?

Beau's Reply

Sir, when I flew to seize the bird
  In spite of your command,
A louder voice than yours I heard,
  And harder to withstand.

You cried—" Forbear!"—but in my breast
  A mightier cried—" Proceed!"—
'Twas Nature, sir, whose strong behest
  Impelled me to the deed.

If killing birds be such a crime,
  (Which I can hardly see),
What think you, sir, of killing Time
  With verse addressed to me?

WILLIAM COWPER.

The Little Dog's Day

ALL in the town were still asleep,
When the sun came up with a shout and a leap.
In the lonely streets unseen by man,
A little dog danced. And the day began.

All his life he'd been good, as far as he could,
And the poor little beast had done all that he should.
But this morning he swore, by Odin and Thor
And the Canine Valhalla—he'd stand it no more!

So his prayer he got granted—to do just what he
    wanted,
Prevented by none, for the space of one day.
" *Jam incipiebo,*[1] *sedere facebo,*" [2]
In dog-Latin he quoth, " *Euge! sophos! hurray!* "

He fought with the he-dogs, and winked at the she-
    dogs,
A thing that had never been *heard* of before.
" For the stigma of gluttony, I care not a button! "
    he
Cried, and ate all he could swallow—and more.

He took sinewy lumps from the shins of old frumps,
And mangled the errand-boys—when he could get 'em.
He shammed furious *rabies,*[3] and bit all the babies,[3]
And followed the cats up the trees, and then ate 'em!

They thought 'twas the devil was holding a revel,
And sent for the parson to drive him away;

---

[1] Now we're off.
[2] I'll make them sit up.
[3] Pronounce either to suit rhyme.

For the town never knew such a hullabaloo
As that little dog raised—till the end of that day.

When the blood-red sun had gone burning down,
And the lights were lit in the little town,
Outside, in the gloom of the twilight grey,
The little dog died when he'd had his day.

RUPERT BROOKE.

The Pekinese National Anthem

THE Pekinese
Disdain to please
  On any set design,
But make a thrall
Of one and all
  By simple Right Divine.

The Pekinese
Our houses seize
  And mould them till they suit,
For every one
's Napoleon
  And Wellington to boot.

The Pekinese
Demosthenes
  Requires no voice to plead:
Those shining eyes,
So soft, so wise,
  Get everything they need.

The Pekinese
Abstain from fleas
  And doggy things like that,

But hate it when
Unthinking men
  Compare them to the cat.

The Pekinese
From autumn trees
  Their colour scheme obtain ;
And all their lives
Their frugal wives
  From any change refrain.

The Pekinese
Have feathered knees,
  And plumes where tails should be,
And as they race
About the place
  They ripple like the sea.

The Pekinese,
Although such wees,
  Are destitute of fear ;
Both fleet and strong,
They bound along,
  As buoyant as the deer.

The Pekinese
Say " Bread and cheese
  Will do for such as you ;
For us a fare
More choice and rare,
  And jolly punctual too."

The Pekinese
Adore their ease
  And slumber like the dead ;

In comfort curled
They view the world
　　As one unending bed.

The Pekinese
On China's seas
　　Embarked to win the West ;
A piece of Ming
's a lovely thing,
　　But oh ! the dogs are best.
E. V. LUCAS.

XVI

GAMES, LEISURE AND HOLIDAYS

The Big Trout

PULL up the ryepecks! Push her home!
  It's roses all the way!
Let garlands lie on Thames's foam—
  A trout has died to-day!
Room for the victor—ho, there, room!
  Who calls the gods to scan
No halfling of the lilied gloom,
  But that leviathan!

Anew (with jostling words unstayed)
  We fight it, inch by inch,
From the first moment when he made
  The line scream off the winch;
'Twas so we struck, we held him so
  Lest weed had triumph wrecked;
Thus to his leap the point dropped low,
  And thus a rush was checked.

O sought-for prize! Full many a day
  The old black punt has swung
Beyond his stance, in twilights grey,
  Or when the dawn was young;
What hopes were ours, what heartbeats high
  Have thrilled us, when he rolled
Up from the jade-green deep, a-nigh,
  Dull-gleaming as of gold!

Glide on, ye stately swans, with grace—
  Ye ne'er again shall see
His headlong dash among the dace
  Beneath the willow-tree;

Ye little bleak, lift up your heads,
  Ye gudgeons, skip at score,
The run between the lily beds
  Shall know its lord no more !

Yet, while exalted pulses stir,
  Regret takes hands with Pride,
Regret for that most splendid spur—
  The Wish Ungratified ;
With hammering heart that bulk I con,
  That spread of tail and fin,
And sigh, like him of Macedon,
  With no more worlds to win.

Pull up the ryepecks, can't you, Jim !
  It's roses all the way !
But ne'er another fish like him
  For any other day !
Room for the victor—look, there, room !
  Who calls the gods to scan
No halfling of the amber gloom.
  But that leviathan !

P. R. CHALMERS.

To an Old Bat

When Vesper trails her gown of grey
  Across the lawn at six or seven
The diligent observer may
  (Or may not) see, athwart the heaven,
An aimless rodent on the wing. Well that
  Is (probably) a Bat . . .
  In any case I shall not sing of that.

O Willow, in our hours of ease
   (That is to say, throughout the Winter),
I take you sometimes on my knees,
   And careless of the frequent splinter,
Caress you tenderly, and sigh, and say,
     " Ye Gods, how long till May ? "

And so as soon as April's here
   I do not sob for Spring to show its
Pale daffodils and all the dear
   Old flowers that keep the minor poets ;
I sing it just because a month (about)
     Will find *you* fairly out.

Revered, beloved, O you whose job
   Is but to serve throughout the season—
To make, if so it be, the Blob,
   And not, (thank heaven !) to ask the reason—
To stand, like Mrs. Hemans' little friend,
     Undoubting to the end.

Old Willow, what a tale to tell—
   Our steady rise, from small beginnings,
Ab ovo usque—usque—well,
   To eighty-four, our highest innings ;
(Ah me, that crowded hour of glorious lives—
     Ten of them, all from drives !)

Once only have you let me in,
   Through all the knocks we've had together ;
That time when, wanting four to win,
   I fairly tried to tonk the leather—
And lo ! a full-faced welt, without the least
     Warning, went S.S.E.

A painful scene. In point of fact
　　I'm doubtful if I ought to hymn it ;
Enough to say you went and cracked,
　　And left me thinkings like " Dimmit "
(And not like " Dimmit ") as I heard Slip call
　　　" Mine ! " and he pouched the ball.

Do you remember, too, the game
　　One August somewhere down in Dorset
When, being told to force the same,
　　We straightway started in to force it. . . .
For half an hour or so we saw it through,
　　And scratched a priceless two ;

Or how the prayer to play for keeps
　　And hang the runs, we didn't need 'em,
So stirred us, we collected heaps
　　With rather more than usual freedom :
Fifty in fourteen minutes—till a catch
　　Abruptly closed the match ?
　　　　* * * * *
Well, well—the coming years (if fine)
　　Shall see us going even stronger ;
So pouring out the oil and wine,
　　Let's sit and drink a little longer :
Here's to a decent average of ten !
　　　(Yours is the oil. Say when . . .)

————

When Morning on the heels of Night
　　Picks up her shroud at five and after,
The diffident observer might
　　(Or might not) see, beneath a rafter,
A pensive rodent upside down. Well that
　　　Is (possibly) a Bat. . . .
In any case I have not sung of that.

A. A. MILNE.

George Hirst

WHEN I faced the bowling of Hirst
I ejaculated, " Do your worst ! "
He said, " Right you are, Sid."
———— And he did.

E. C. BENTLEY.

To My First Catch

(*in immediate prospect*)

COME not as, if I recollect aright,
You came last year, with sudden-soaring flight
Rising, and falling from a monstrous height,

Where I, (that am not fond of fielding deep
Thus early), struck all over of a heap,
Watched with pained eyes, and gauged your down-
    ward sweep,

And raised beseeching hands to clutch you round,
Whence you escaped, and with one mad rebound
Insanely dashed yourself upon the ground.

Not from the bat's edge come, with that weird swerve
By golfers called the slice, whose double curve
Foils the keen eye and shocks the high-strung nerve ;

Nor in the slips approach me, with a spin
That grinds you from the palm before you're in—
And oh, if straight I stand, or square, or thin,

Whate'er my post, in whatsoever wise
You come, I trust I may at least devise
Some plausible excuse, if need should rise.

That either I may urge : " Good Such-an-one,
Almost I had it, but I was undone
By the surpassing glory of the Sun " ;

Or haply, " See, how slippery lies the grass ;
How dark yon tree, wherein the ball did pass
Clean from my ken ; Good Captain," or " Alas,

" Good Bowler, blame me not ; such happening
Had failed the most elect ; our very King
(God bless him !) would have missed the silly thing,"

And, if this ordeal must needs befall ;
If I see no excuse, however small,
Likely to serve ; why then, confound it all,

Come in no gentle shape ; but come, and be
The Catch Impossible—too fierce to see,
Too far to reach—it makes no odds to me ;

That I, with one wild leap upon the sward,
May stretch a hand (the left for choice) and lord !
May find you sticking of your own accord

Warm in the palm ; and after one hushed sigh,
Rabble and connoisseur alike shall cry
" A miracle ! a miracle ! "—while I

Lightly may toss you from me, with an air
Of one that holds so paltry an affair
Mere commonplace ; or, even if my pray'r

Lack fulness, if this glory be denied,
I yet may glean a melancholy pride
In the condoning tribute of, " Well tried ! "

MAJOR JOHN KENDALL.

The Sea

THERE are certain things—a spider, a ghost,
  The income-tax, gout, an umbrella for three—
That I hate, but the thing that I hate the most
  Is a thing they call the SEA.

Pour some salt water over the floor—
  Ugly I'm sure you'll allow it to be :
Suppose it extended a mile or more,
  That's very like the SEA.

Beat a dog till it howls outright—
  Cruel, but all very well for a spree :
Suppose that one did so day and night,
  That would be like the SEA.

I had a vision of nursery-maids ;
  Tens of thousands passed by me—
All leading children with wooden spades,
  And this was by the SEA.

Who invented those spades of wood ?
  Who was it cut them out of the tree ?
None, I think, but an idiot could—
  Or one that loved the SEA.

It is pleasant and dreamy, no doubt, to float
  With " thoughts as boundless, and souls as free " ;
But suppose you are very unwell in a boat.
  How do you like the SEA ?

There is an insect that people avoid
  (Whence is derived the verb " to flee ")

P

Where have you been by it most annoyed
　　In lodgings by the SEA.

If you like coffee with sand for dregs,
　　A decided hint of salt in your tea,
And a fishy taste in the very eggs—
　　By all means choose the SEA.

And if, with these dainties to drink and eat,
　　You prefer not a vestige of grass or tree,
And a chronic state of wet in your feet,
　　Then—I recommend the SEA.

For *I* have friends who dwell by the coast,
　　Pleasant friends they are to me !
It is when I with them I wonder most
　　That anyone likes the SEA.

They take me a walk : though tired and stiff,
　　To climb the heights I madly agree :
And, after a tumble or so from the cliff,
　　They kindly suggest the SEA.

I try the rocks, and I think it cool,
　　That they laugh with such an excess of glee,
As I heavily slip into every pool
　　That skirts the cold, cold SEA.

LEWIS CARROLL.

206

Bangkolidye

"Gimme my scarlet tie,"
Says I.

" Gimme my brownest boots and hat,
Gimme a vest with a pattern fancy,
Gimme a gel with some style, like Nancy,
And then—well, it's gimes as I'll be at,
Seein' as its bangkolidye,"
Says I.

" May miss it, but we'll try,"
Says I.

Nancy ran like a frightened 'en
Hup the steps of the bloomin' styeshun.
Bookin'-orfus at last ! Salvyeshun !
An' the two returns was five-and-ten.
" An' travellin' mikes your money fly,"
Says I.

" This atmosphere is 'igh,"
Says I.

Twelve in a carriage is pretty thick,
When 'ite of the twelve is a sittin', smokin' ;
Nancy started 'er lawkin' and jokin',
Syin' she 'oped as we shouldn't be sick ;
" Don't go on, or you'll mike me die ! "
Says I.

" Three styeshuns we've porst by,"
Says I.

" So hout we get at the next, my gel."
When we got hout, she were pale and saint-like,
White in the gills, and sorter faint-like,
An' said my cigaw 'ad a powerful smell,
" Well, it's the sime as I always buy,"
Says I.

" 'Ites them clouds in the sky,"

Says I.

" Don't like 'em at all, that's flat—
Black as your boots and sorter thick'nin'."
" If it's wet," says she, " it *will* be sick'nin'.
I wish as I'd brought my other 'at."
" You thinks too much of your finery,"

Says I.

" Keep them sanwidjus dry,"

Says I,

When the rine came down in a reggiler sheet.
But what can yo do with one umbrella,
And a damp gel strung on the arm of a fella ?
" Well, rined-on 'am ain't pleasant to eat,
If yer don't believe it, just go an' try,"

Says I.

" There is some gels whort cry,"

Says I.

" And there is some don't shed a tear,
But just get tempers, and when they has 'em
Reaches a p'int in their sarcasem,
As on'y a dorg could bear to 'ear."
This unto Nancy by-and-by,

Says I.

All's hover now. And why,

Says I.

But why did I wear them boots, that vest ?
The bloom is off 'em ; they're sad to see ;
And hev'rythin's off twixt Nancy and me ;
And my trousers is off and gone to be pressed—
And ain't this a blimed bangkolidye ?

Says I.

BARRY PAIN.

The Schoolmaster Abroad

(The Steam-Yacht "Argonaut" was chartered from Messrs. Perowne & Lunn by a body of Public School Masters for the purposes of an educative visit to the Levant)

O " ISLES " (as Byron said) " of Greece ! "
   For which the firm of Homer sang,
Especially that little piece
   Interpreted by Mr. Lang ;
Where the unblushing Sappho wrote
The hymns we hardly like to quote ;—

I cannot share his grave regret
   Who found your fame had been and gone ;
There seems to be a future yet
   For Tenedos and Marathon ;
Fresh glory gilds their deathless sun,
And this is due to Dr. Lunn !

What though your harpers twang no more ?
   What though your various lyres are dumb ?
See where by Cirrha's sacred shore,
   Bold Argonauts, the Ushers come !
All bring their maps and some their wives,
And at the vision Greece revives !

The Delphic oracles are off,
   But still the site is always there ;
The fumes that made the Pythian cough
   Still permeate the conscious air ;
Parnassus, of the arduous " grade,"
May still be climbed, with local aid.

Lunching upon the self-same rock
　　Whence Xerxes viewed the wine-red frith,
They realize with vivid shock
　　The teachings of " the smaller Smith ";
With bated breath they murmur—" This
Is actually Salamis ! "

They visit where Penelope
　　Nightly unwove the work of day,
Staving her suitors off till he,
　　Ulysses, let the long-bow play,
And on his brave grass-widow's breast
Forgot Calypso and the rest.

In Crete, where Theseus first embraced
　　His Ariadne, they explore
(Just now authentically traced)
　　The footprints of the Minotaur ;
And follow, to the maze's source,
The thread of some profound discourse.

That isle where Leto, sick with fright,
　　So scandalized her mortal kin,
Where young Apollo, lord of light,
　　Commenced his progress as a twin—
Fair Delos, they shall get to know,
And Paros, where the marbles grow.

Not theirs the course of crude delight
　　On which the common tourist wends ;
From faith they move, by way of sight,
　　To knowledge meant for noble ends ;
'Twill be among their purest joys
To work it off upon the boys.

One hears the travelled teacher call
　　Upon the Upper Fifth to note
(Touching the Spartan counter-wall)
　　How great the lore of Mr. Grote ;
And tell them, " His are just the views
I formed myself—at Syracuse ! "

When Jones is at a loss to show
　　Where certain islands ought to be,
How well to whack him hard and low
　　And say, " The pain is worse for me,
To whom the Cyclades are quite
Familiar, like the Isle of Wight."

And then the lecture after prep. !
　　The Magic Lantern's lurid slide !
The speaker pictured on the step
　　Of some old shrine, with no inside ;
Or groping on his reverent knees
For Eleusinian mysteries !

Hellas defunct ?　O say not so,
　　While Public School-boys faint to hear
The tales of antique love or woe,
　　Brought home and rendered strangely clear
With instantaneous Kodak-shots
Secured by Ushers on the spots !
SIR OWEN SEAMAN.

The Visitors' Book, Hartland Quay

CORYDON.　What, Echo, shall I find at Hartland
　　　　Quay,
　　Save walls abandoned long ago, and sea ?
ECHO.　　　　　　　　　　　Go and see.

CORYDON. Nay, but describe it, Echo, for thy sighs
  My roving accents quaintly parodize.
ECHO.   Paradise.
CORYDON. How shall I reach (for wind and wave
    are fickle)
  Those fields untouched by harrow or by sickle?
ECHO.   Bicycle.
CORYDON. What of the beds? What portion waits
    the roamer,
  Lulled by the murmur of the Atlantic comber?
ECHO.   Coma.
CORYDON. What of the food? What influence
    supreme,
  If baby seems in pain, will hush a scream?
ECHO.   Luscious cream.
CORYDON. And will this land, where nought that's
    tender grows,
  Yield beans and blackberries αὐτομάτως?
ECHO.   Or tomatoes.
CORYDON. What exploits, then, shall occupy my
    time,
  Wearied with wandering in many a clime?
ECHO.   Many a climb.
CORYDON. Were it not best to lie on couch of
    clover?
  Great is the peril, lest I should fall over?
ECHO.   Faugh! Loafer!
CORYDON. If, yet untired, I'd cool the heated
    limb,
  Can any panacea heal this whim?
ECHO.   A healthy swim.
CORYDON. What then my week's expenditure, and
    how
  Reckoned the cost, my mind enlighten now.
ECHO.   Light enow.

CORYDON.   What of mine host ? for, if the host be
        rude,
    The fare, whate'er it be, is none so good.
ECHO.   None's so good.
CORYDON.   Come, Echo, thou hast visited this spot ?
    I have conjectured shrewdly, have I not ?
ECHO.   Have I not !
CORYDON.   Who dwelt with thee, where Hartland
        lies concealed ;
    Where winds, that rule in sea, spare stone and field ?
ECHO.   Rieu, Lindsay, Speyer, Stone, and Field.
CORYDON.   What is thy name ? For Attic moun-
        tains make a
    Clear Ἥχω, but thou art in Pindar Ἄχα.
ECHO.   R.A.K.

R. A. KNOX.

The First Tee

(Mullion)

IT is the place, it is the place, my soul !
    (Blow bugle, blow ; sing triangle ; toot, fife !)
Down to the sea the close-cropped pastures roll,
Couches behind yon sandy hill the goal
    Whereat, it may be, after ceaseless strife
The " Colonel " shall find peace, and Henry say,
        " Your hole " . . .

    Caddie, give me my driver, caddie,
        The sun shines hot, but there's half a breeze,
    Enough to rustle the tree-tops, laddie,
        Only supposing there were some trees ;
    The year's at the full and the morn's at eleven,
    It's a wonderful day just straight from heaven,
    And this is a hole I can do in seven—
            Caddie, my driver, please.

213

Three times a day from now till Monday week
   (Ten peerless days in all) I take my stand
Vestured in some *degagé* mode of breek
(The chess-board touch, with squares that almost
      speak),
   And lightly sketch my Slice into the Sand,
As based on bigger men, but much of it unique . . .

   Caddie, give me my driver, caddie,
     Note my style on the first few tees ;
   Duncan fashioned my wrist-work, laddie,
     Taylor taught me to twist my knees ;
I've a beautiful swing that I learnt from Vardon
(I practise it sometimes down the garden—
" My fault ! Sorry ! I *beg* your pardon ! ")—
      Caddie, my driver, please.

Only ten little days, in which to do
   So much ! E.g. the twelfth ; ah, it was there
The Secretary met his Waterloo
But perished gamely, playing twenty-two ;
   His clubs (*ten little days !*) lie bleaching where
Sea-poppies blow (*ten days !*) and wheeling sea-birds
     mew . . .

   Caddie, give me my driver, caddie,
     Let us away with thoughts like these ;
   A week and a half is a lifetime, laddie,
     The day that's here is the day to seize ;
Carpe diem—yes, that's the motto,
" Work be jiggered ! " and likewise " What ho ! "
I'M NOT GOING BACK TILL I'VE JOLLY WELL GOT TO !
      Caddie, my driver, please.
               A. A. MILNE.

The Seventh Hole

Now let the natural choir
Its tuneful song uplift ;
Bang the field-piece, twang the lyre,
If any have that gift ;
Now let the young lambs bound
As to the tabor's sound ;
In fact, let every living thing be glad,
Go it like fun,
And carry on like mad ;
Metre and rhyme be blowed
Save as they come my way ;
I cannot interrupt my ode
For trifles such as they ;
Because, to put the matter in a word,
My heart, my heart, is like a singing bird ;
Because this blessed morning I have done
The seventh hole in one.

It did not look like that at first at all ;
I sliced the beastly ball,
Which swerved from off the club
Towards about the worst spot in a round half-mile,
Furze, heather, some abominable grass and general
    scrub,
Immeasurably vile.
But, even as distraction filled my breast,
The decent gods were kind.
The wind, the jolly old convenient wind,
Flew up and showed a sudden interest ;
Triumphantly o'ercame that fatal cut,
But
Blew the vain ball towards a frightful bunker,
A regular funker.

Then, as I lifted up my cry, " Alas ! "
(Premature ass !)
My beautiful, my lovely ball
Landed a trifle short, and, instead of running on into
    that perfect funker
Of a bunker,
Pitched bang upon a very small
Obtruding scrap of rock,
And bounced into the air like one o'clock.
O wind that swept my ball from wild despair,
O rock that sent it flying in the air,
Be happy : once my luck has smiled on me.

Saved from the pit, I breathed anew,
And it was at that moment,
E'en as I gazed into the blue
To watch the wild ball as it flew,
That my irate opponent
(If you'll forgive that ——*m*)
So far forgot his high traditional phlegm
As to remark, " Good stroke ! "
Sarcastically, mind you, not in joke,
So that whatever happened served *him* right.
And things did happen, that I own.
Kicked by that favouring stone,
The high ball, going strong and free
Up in the air some thirty feet,
Went slap against a lofty tree
(How sweet ! How sweet !)
And leapt (a really thrilling sight)
Off, at an angle rarely to be seen,
For the first time more or less in the direction of the
    green.
O stone that gave my ball a needful kick,
O tree that sent it flying back darned quick,
Live ever : twice my luck has smiled on me.

216

There is a bank that rims the green around,
A dangerous bank, where trouble oft is found;
On this my ball came down a hearty smack,
Tore around its entire length at a terrific pace,
Like a winning car on the steepest part of the Brook-
    lands track,
And, ultimately rushing off its glissome face,
Hurtled full lick for the hole . . . And then . . .
O tree that helped the ball towards the pin,
O flag that stopped it dead and put it in,
Stand stoutly; thrice my luck has smiled on me.
For so it was. Once in an age or so
The gods bring off their wonders. That is all
I know on earth, and all I want to know.
The ball was in the tin, and I had done
The seventh hole in one.

Then to my foe, who stood with drooping head,
" That for a half," I said.

MAJOR JOHN KENDALL.

The Path to Rome

In these boots, and with this staff
Two hundred leaguers and a half
Walked I, went I, paced I, tripped I,
Marched I, held I, skelped I, slipped I,
Pushed I, panted, swung and dashed I;
Picked I, forded, swam and splashed I,
Strolled I, climbed I, crawled and scrambled,
Dropped and dipped I, ranged and rambled;
Plodded I, hobbled I, trudged and tramped I,
And in lonely spinnies camped I,
And in haunted pinewoods slept I,
Lingered, loitered, limped and crept I,
Clambered, halted, stepped and leapt I;

Slowly sauntered, roundly strode I,
And . . .   (Oh! Patron saints and Angels
                That protect the four evangels!
                And you Prophets vel majores
                Vel incerti, vel minores,
                Virgines ac confessores
                Chief of whose peculiar glories
                Est in Aula Regis stare
                Atque orare et exorare
                Et clamare et conclamare
                Clamantes cum clamoribus
                Pro nobis peccatoribus).

Let me not conceal it . . . Rode I.
(For who but critics could complain
Of " riding " in a railway train ?)
Across the valleys and the high-land
With all the world on either hand,
Drinking when I had a mind to,
Singing when I felt inclined to ;
Nor ever turned my face to home
Till I had slaked my heart at Rome.

                HILAIRE BELLOC.

The Strenuous Life

On the cabin-roof I lie
Gazing into vacancy.
Make no noise and break no jest,
I am peaceful and at rest.

Somewhere back in days gone by
I did something—was it I ?
Do not ask : I have forgot
Whether it was I or not.

Sometime I may have to do
Something else ; but so may you.
Do not argue, but admit
That we need not think of it.

Thought has ever been my foe ;
That is so. Yes. That is so.
On the cabin-roof I lie
Gazing into vacancy.

A. H. SIDGWICK.

XVII

STUDIES IN DEJECTION

Q

Ode—"On a Distant Prospect" of Making a Fortune

Now the " rosy morn appearing "
  Floods with light the dazzling heaven ;
And the schoolboy groans on hearing
  That eternal clock strike seven :—
Now the waggoner is driving
  Tow'rds the fields his clattering wain ;
Now the blue-bottle, reviving,
  Buzzes down his native pane.

But to me the morn is hateful :
  Wearily I stretch my legs,
Dress, and settle to my plateful
  Of (perhaps inferior) eggs.
Yesterday Miss Crump, by message,
  Mentioned " rent," which " p'raps I'd pay " ;
And I have a dismal presage
  That she'll call, herself, to-day.

Once, I breakfasted off rosewood,
  Smoked through silver-mounted pipes—
Then how my patrician nose would
  Turn up at the thought of " swipes ! "
Ale,—occasionally claret,—
  Graced my luncheon then ;—and now
I drink porter in a garret,
  To be paid for heaven knows how.

When the evening shades are deepened,
  And I doff my hat and gloves,
No sweet bird is there to " cheep and
  Twitter twenty million loves " ;

No dark-ringleted canaries
　　Sing to me of " hungry foam " ;
No imaginary " Marys "
　　Call fictitious " cattle home."

Araminta, sweetest, fairest !
　　Solace once of every ill !
How I wonder if thou bearest
　　Mivins in remembrance still !
If that Friday night is banished
　　From a once retentive mind,
When the others somehow vanished,
　　And we two were left behind :—

When in accents low, yet thrilling,
　　I did all my love declare ;
Mentioned that I'd not a shilling—
　　Hinted that we need not care :
And complacently you listened
　　To my somewhat long address,
And I thought the tear that glistened
　　In the downdropt eye said Yes.

Once, a happy child, I carolled
　　O'er green lawns the whole day through,
Not unpleasingly apparelled
　　In a tightish suit of blue :—
What a change has now passed o'er me !
　　Now with what dismay I see
Every rising morn before me !
　　Goodness gracious patience me !

And I'll prowl, a moodier Lara,
　　Thro' the world, as prowls the bat,
And habitually wear a
　　Cypress wreath around my hat :
224

And when Death snuffs out the taper
　Of my Life (as soon he must),
I'll send up to every paper,
　" Died, T. Mivins ; of disgust."

C. S. CALVERLEY.

Oxford Re-visited

I WANDERED down the Broad and up the High,
　As I was wont, in far off days, to do—
　When lo, debouching from The Grid came two
Resplendent youths who, sauntering idly by,
Cast on my form a supercilious eye,
　Whose glance said very plainly, " Who are you
　That dare obtrude yourself upon our view ?
The place is ours, for we have bought it.　Fly ! "
I realized that I was on the shelf
　In that brief moment : saddened and forlorn
　　I paused irresolute upon my way :
Then, thinking that a dog soon has his day,
　Strode on, till suddenly I found myself
　　　Standing (like Ruth) " amid the alien Corn."

HARTLEY CARRICK.

XVIII

SOCIAL AFFAIRS

The Talented Man

A Letter from a Lady in London to a Lady at Lausanne

DEAR Alice, you'll laugh when you know it,—
  Last week, at the Duchess's ball,
I danced with clever new poet,—
  You've heard of him,—Tully St. Paul.
Miss Jonquil was perfectly frantic :
  I wish you had seen Lady Anne !
It really was very romantic,
  He *is* such a talented man !

He came up from Brazennose College,
  Just caught, as they call it, this spring ;
And his head, love, is stuffed full of knowledge
  Of every conceivable thing.
Of science and logic he chatters,
  As fine and as fast as he can ;
Although I'm no judge of such matters,
  I'm sure he's a talented man.

His stories and jests are delightful :—
  Not stories or jests, dear, for you ;
The jests are exceedingly spiteful,
  The stories not always *quite* true.
Perhaps to be kind and veracious
  May do pretty well at Lausanne ;
But it never would answer,—good gracious !
  Chez nous—in a talented man.

He sneers,—how my Alice would scold him !—
  At the bliss of a sigh or a tear ;
He laughed—only think !—when I told him
  How we cried o'er Trevelyan last year ;

I vow I was quite in a passion ;
  I broke all the sticks of my fan ;
But sentiment's quite out of fashion,
  It seems, in a talented man.

Lady Bab, who is terribly moral,
  Has told me that Tully is vain,
And apt,—which is silly—to quarrel,
  And fond—which is sad—of champagne.
I listened and doubted, dear Alice,
  For I saw, when my Lady began,
It was only the dowager's malice :—
  She *does* hate a talented man !

He's hideous, I own it. But fame, love,
  Is all that these eyes can adore :
He's lame,—but Lord Byron was lame, love,
  And dumpy,—but so is Tom Moore.
Then his voice,—*such* a voice ! my sweet creature,
  It's like your Aunt Lucy's toucan ;
But oh ! what's a tone or a feature,
  When once one's a talented man ?

My mother, you know, all the season,
  Has talked of Sir Geoffrey's estate ;
And truly, to do the fool reason,
  He *has* been less horrid of late,
But to-day, when we drive in the carriage,
  I'll tell her to lay down her plan :—
If ever I venture on marriage,
  It must be a talented man !

P.S.—I have found, on reflection,
  One fault in my friend,—*entre nous* :
Without it, he'd just be perfection :—
  Poor fellow, he has not a *sou* !

And so, when he comes in September
  To shoot with my uncle, Sir Dan,
I've promised mamma to remember
  He's *only* a talented man !

W. M. PRAED.

Mrs. Mary Blaize

GOOD people all, with one accord,
  Lament for Madam Blaize,
Who never wanted a good word—
  From those who spoke her praise.

The needy seldom pass'd her door,
  And always found her kind ;
She freely lent to all the poor—
  Who left a pledge behind.

She strove the neighbourhood to please
  With manners wondrous winning ;
And never followed wicked ways—
  Unless when she was sinning.

At church, in silks and satins new,
  With hoop of monstrous size,
She never slumbered in her pew—
  But when she shut her eyes.

Her love was sought, I do aver,
  By twenty beaux and more ;
The King himself has followed her—
  When she has walk'd before.

But now, her wealth and finery fled,
  Her hangers-on cut short-all :
The doctors found, when she was dead,—
  Her last disorder mortal.

Let us lament, in sorrow sore,
  For Kent Street well may say,
That had she lived a twelvemonth more,—
  She had not died to-day.

OLIVER GOLDSMITH.

Blue Blood

SPURN not the nobly born
  With love affected,
Nor treat with virtuous scorn
  The well-connected.
High rank involves no shame—
We boast an equal claim
With him of humble name
  To be respected !
    Blue blood ! Blue blood !
      When virtuous love is sought,
      Thy power is naught,
      Though dating from the Flood,
      Blue blood !

Spare us the bitter pain
  Of stern denials,
Nor with low-born disdain
  Augment our trials.
Hearts just as pure and fair
May beat in Belgrave Square
As in the lowly air
  Of Seven Dials !

Blue blood! Blue blood!
　Of what avail art thou
　To serve me now?
Though dating from the Flood,
　Blue blood!

SIR W. S. GILBERT.

Precious Stones

MY cherrystones! I prize them,
　No tongue can tell how much!
Each lady caller eyes them,
　And madly longs to touch!
At eve I lift them down, I look
　Upon them, and I cry;
Recalling how my Prince "partook"
　(Sweet word) of cherry-pie!

To me it was an Era
　In life, that Dejeuner!
They ate, they sipped Madeira
　Much in the usual way.
Many a soft item would there be,
　No doubt, upon the carte:
But one made life a heaven to me:
　It was a cherry-tart.

Lightly the spoonfuls entered
　That mouth on which the gaze
Of ten fair girls was centred
　In rapturous amaze.
Soon that august assemblage cleared
　The dish: and—as they ate—
The stones, all coyly, re-appeared
　On each illustrious plate.

And when His Royal Highness
   Withdrew to take the air,
Waiving our natural shyness,
   We swooped upon his chair.
Policemen at our garments clutched :
   We mocked those feeble powers ;
And soon the treasures that had touched
   Exalted lips were ours !

One large one—at the moment
   It seemed almost divine—
Was got by that Miss Beaumont :
   And three, O three, are mine !
Yes, the three stones that rest beneath
   Glass, on that plain deal shelf,
Stranger, once dallied with the teeth
   Of Royalty itself.

Let Parliament abolish
   Churches and States and Thrones,
With reverent hand I'll polish
   Still, still my Cherrystones.
A clod—a piece of orange-peel—
   An end of a cigar—
Once trod on by a princely heel,
   How beautiful they are !

Years since, I climbed Saint Michael
   His Mount :—you'll all go there
Of course, and those who like'll
   Sit in Saint Michael's Chair :
For there I saw, within a frame,
   The pen—O heavens ! the pen—
With which a Duke had signed his name,
   And other gentlemen.

" Great among geese," I faltered,
    " Is she who grew that quill ! "
And Deathless Bird, unaltered
    Is mine opinion still.
Yet sometimes, as I view my three
    Stones with a thoughtful brow,
I think there possibly might be
    E'en greater geese than thou.

C. S. CALVERLEY.

Our Village.—By a Villager

OUR village, that's to say not Miss Mitford's village,
    but our village of Bullock Smithy,
Is come into by an avenue of trees, three oak
    pollards, two elders and a withy ;
And in the middle there's a green of about not
    exceeding an acre and a half ;
It's common to all, and fed off by nineteen cows,
    six ponies, three horses, five asses, two foals,
    seven pigs and a calf.
Besides a pond in the middle, which is held by a
    similar sort of common law lease,
And contains twenty ducks, six drakes, three ganders,
    two dead dogs, four drowned kittens, and twelve
    geese.
Of course the green's cropt very close, and does famous
    for bowling when the little village boys play at
    cricket ;
Only some horse or pig, or cow, or great jackass, is
    sure to come and stand right before the wicket ;
There's fifty-five private houses, let alone barns and
    workshops and pigstyes and poultry huts and
    such-like sheds ;

With plenty of public-houses—two Foxes, one Green
    Man, three Bunch of Grapes, one Crown, and
    six King's Heads.
The Green Man is reckoned the best, as the only one
    that for love or money can raise
A postilion, a blue jacket, two deplorable lame white
    horses, and a ramshackled " neat post-chaise."
There's one parish church for all the people, what-
    soever may be their ranks in life or their degrees,
Except one very damp, small, dark, freezing-cold
    Methodist Chapel of Ease ;
And close by the churchyard there's a stone-mason's
    yard, that when the time is seasonable
Will furnish with afflictions sore and marble urns
    and cherubims very cheap and reasonable ;
There's a cage, comfortable enough, I've been in it
    with old Jack Jeffreys and Tom Pike ;
For the Green Man next door will send you in ale,
    gin, or anything else you like ;
I can't speak of the stocks, as nothing remains of
    them but the upright post,
But the Pound is kept in repair for the sake of Cob's
    horse, as is always there almost ;
There's a smithy of course, where that queer sort of
    a chap in his way, old Joe Bradley,
Perpetually hammers and stammers, for he stutters
    and shoes horses very badly.
There's a shop of sorts, that sells everything, kept
    by the widow of Mr. Task.
But when you go there, it's ten to one she's out of
    everything you ask ;
You'll know her house by the swarm of boys, like
    flies, about the old sugary cask ;
There are six empty houses, and not so well papered
    inside as out ;

For the billstickers won't beware, but stick notices
  of sales and election placards all about ;
There's the Doctor's with a green door, where the
  garden pots in the windows are seen,
A weakly monthly rose that won't blow, and a dead
  geranium, and a tea-plant with five black leaves
  and one green.
As for hollyoaks at the cottage doors, and honey-
  suckles and jasmines, you may go and whistle ;
But the Tailor's front garden grows two cabbages, a
  dock, a ha'porth of pennyroyal, two dandelions,
  and a thistle.
There are three small orchards—Mr. Busby's the
  schoolmaster's is the chief—
With two pear-trees that don't bear ; one plum and
  an apple, that every year is stripped by a thief.
There's another small day-school too, kept by the
  respectable Mrs. Gaby.
A select establishment, for six little boys and one
  big, and four little girls and a baby ;
There's a rectory, with pointed gables and strange
  odd chimneys that never smokes,
For the rector don't live on his living like other
  Christian kind of folks ;
There's a barber's once a week filled with rough,
  black-bearded, shock-headed churls,
And a window with two feminine men's heads, and
  two masculine ladies in false curls ;
There's a butcher's, and a carpenter's, and a plumber's
  and a small greengrocer's and a baker,
But he won't bake on Sunday, and there's a sexton
  that's a coal-merchant besides, and an under-
  taker ;
And a toyshop, but not a whole one, for a village
  can't compare with the London shops ;

R   237

One window sells drums, dolls, kites, carts, bats,
    Clout's balls, and the other sells malt and hops.
And Mrs. Brown, in domestic economy not to be a
    bit behind her betters,
Lets her house to a milliner, a watchmaker, a rat-
    catcher, a cobbler, lives in it herself, and it's
    the post-office for letters.
Now I've gone through all the village—aye, from
    end to end, save and except one more house,
But I haven't come to that—and I hope I never
    shall—and that's the Village Poor House !

THOMAS HOOD.

The Bath

BROAD is the Gate and wide the Path
That leads man to his daily bath ;
But ere you spend the shining hour
With plunge and spray, with sluice and show'r–
With all that teaches you to dread
The bath as little as your bed—
Remember, whereso'er you be,
To shut the door and turn the key !

I had a friend—my friend no more !—
Who failed to bolt the bath-room door ;

A maiden aunt of his, one day,
Walked in, as half-submerged he lay !

She did not notice nephew John,
And turned the boiling water on !

He had no time, or even scope,
To camouflage himself with soap,
But gave a yell and flung aside
The sponge 'neath which he sought to hide !

238

It fell to earth I know not where!
He beat his breast in his despair,

And then, like Venus from the foam,
Sprang into view, and made for home!

His aunt fell fainting to the ground!
Alas! they never brought her round!

She died, intestate, in her prime,
The victim of another's crime;

And John can never quite forget
How, by a breach of etiquette,
He lost, at one fell swoop (or plunge),
His aunt, his honour, and his sponge!

CAPTAIN HARRY GRAHAM.

Lord Finchley

LORD FINCHLEY tried to mend the Electric Light
Himself.
It struck him dead: And serve him right!
It is the business of the wealthy man
To give employment to the artisan.

HILAIRE BELLOC.

Etiquette

THE *Ballyshannon* foundered off the coast of Cariboo,
And down in fathoms many went the captain and the
crew;
Down went the owners—greedy men whom hope of
gain allured:
Oh, dry the starting tear, for they were heavily
insured.

Besides the captain and the mate, the owners and the
    crew,
The passengers were also drowned excepting only
    two ;
Young Peter Gray, who tasted teas for Baker, Croop
    and Co.,
And Somers, who from Eastern shores imported
    indigo.

These passengers, by reason of their clinging to a
    mast,
Upon a desert island were eventually cast.
They hunted for their meals, as Alexander Selkirk
    used,
But they could not chat together—they had not
    been introduced.

For Peter Gray, and Somers too, though certainly
    in trade,
Were properly particular about the friends they
    made ;
And somehow thus they settled it without a word of
    mouth—
That Gray should take the northern half, while Somers
    took the south.

On Peter's portion oysters grew—a delicacy rare,
But oysters were a delicacy Peter couldn't bear.
On Somers' side was turtle, on the shingle lying
    thick
Which Somers couldn't eat, because it always made
    him sick.

Gray gnashed his teeth with envy as he saw a mighty
    store
Of turtle unmolested on his fellow-creature's shore :

The oysters at his feet aside impatiently he shoved,
For turtle and his mother were the only things he
loved.

And Somers sighed in sorrow as he settled in the
south,
For the thought of Peter's oysters brought the water
to his mouth.
He longed to lay him down upon the shelly bed, and
stuff :
He had often eaten oysters, but had never had
enough.

How they wished an introduction to each other they
had had
When on board the *Ballyshannon* ! And it drove
them nearly mad
To think how very friendly with each other they
might get,
If it wasn't for the arbitrary rule of etiquette !

One day, when out a-hunting for the *mus ridiculus*,
Gray overheard his fellow-man soliloquizing thus :
" I wonder how the playmates of my youth are
getting on,
M'Connell, S. B. Walters, Paddy Byles, and Robin-
son ? "

These simple words made Peter as delighted as could
be,
Old Chummies at the Charterhouse were Robinson
and he !
He walked straight up to Somers, then he turned
extremely red,
Hesitated, hummed and hawed a bit, then cleared
his throat and said :

" I beg your pardon—pray forgive me if I seem too
    bold,
But you have breathed a name I knew familiarly of
    old.
You spoke aloud of Robinson—I happened to be
    by—
You know him ? " " Yes, extremely well." " Allow
    me—so do I."

It was enough : they felt they could more sociably
    get on,
For (ah, the magic of the fact !) they each knew
    Robinson !
And Mr. Somers' turtle was at Peter's service quite,
And Mr. Somers punished Peter's oyster-beds all night.

They soon became like brothers from community
    of wrongs ;
They wrote each other little odes and sang each
    other songs ;
They told each other anecdotes disparaging their
    wives ;
On several occasions, too, they saved each other's
    lives.

They felt quite melancholy when they parted for
    the night,
And got up in the morning soon as ever it was light ;
Each other's pleasant company they so relied upon,
And all because it happened that they both knew
    Robinson !

They lived for many years on that inhospitable
    shore,
And day by day they learned to love each other
    more and more.

At last, to their astonishment, on getting up one
    day,
They saw a vessel anchored in the offing of the bay !

To Peter an idea occurred.   " Suppose we cross the
    main ?
So good an opportunity may not occur again."
And Somers thought a minute, then ejaculated,
    " Done !
I wonder how my business in the City's getting on ? "

" But stay," said Mr. Peter : " when in England,
    as you know,
I earned a living tasting teas for Baker, Croop, and
    Co.
I may be superseded, my employers think me dead ! "
" Then come with me," said Somers, " and taste
    indigo instead."

But all their plans were scattered in a moment when
    they found
The vessel was a convict ship from Portland, outward
    bound !
When a boat came off to fetch them, though they
    felt it very kind
To go on board they firmly but respectfully declined.

As both the happy settlers roared with laughter at
    the joke,
They recognized an unattractive fellow pulling
    stroke :
'Twas Robinson—a convict, in an unbecoming
    frock !
Condemned to seven years for misappropriating
    stock ! ! !

They laughed no more, for Somers thought he had
    been rather rash
In knowing one whose friend had misappropriated
    cash ;
And Peter thought a foolish tack he must have gone
    upon,
In making the acquaintance of a friend of Robinson.

At first they didn't quarrel very openly, I've heard ;
They nodded when they met, and now and then
    exchanged a word :
The word grew rare, and rarer still the nodding of
    the head,
And when they meet each other now, they cut each
    other dead.

To allocate the island they agreed by word of mouth,
And Peter takes the north again, and Somers takes
    the south :
And Peter has the oysters, which he loathes with
    horror grim,
And Somers has the turtle—turtle disagrees with
    him.

SIR W. S. GILBERT.

Sir Christopher Wren

SIR CHRISTOPHER WREN
Said " I am going to dine with some men ;
If any one calls,
Say I am designing St. Paul's."

E. C. BENTLEY.

Godolphin Horne,

Who was cursed with the Sin of Pride, and became a Boot-black

GODOLPHIN HORNE was Nobly Born ;
He held the Human Race in Scorn,
And lived with all his Sisters where
His Father lived, in Berkeley Square.
And oh ! the Lad was Deathly Proud !
He never shook your Hand or Bowed,
But merely smirked and nodded thus :
How perfectly ridiculous !
Alas ! That such Affected Tricks
Should flourish in a Child of Six !
(For such was Young Godolphin's age).
Just then, the Court required a Page,
Whereat
    The Lord High Chamberlain
(The Kindest and the Best of Men),
He went good-naturedly and took
A Perfectly Enormous Book
Called *People Qualified to Be*
Attendant on His Majesty,
And murmured, as he scanned the list
(To see that no one should be missed),
" There's William Coutts has got the Flue,
And Billy Higgs would never do,
And Guy de Vere is far too young,
And . . . wasn't D'Alton's Father hung ?
And as for Alexander Byng !— . . .
I think I know the kind of thing,
A Churchman, cleanly, nobly born,
Come let us say Godolphin Horne ? "
But hardly had he said the word
When Murmurs of Dissent were heard.

245

The King of Iceland's Eldest Son
Said, " Thank you !   I am taking none !
The Aged Duchess of Athlone
Remarked, in her sub-acid tone,
" I doubt if He is what we need ! "
With which the Bishops all agreed ;
And even Lady Mary Flood
(*So* Kind, and oh ! so *really* good)
Said, " No !   He wouldn't do at all,
He'd make us feel a lot too small."
The Chamberlain said,
　　　　" . . . Well, well, well !
No doubt you're right. . . .   One cannot tell ! "
He took his Gold and Diamond Pen
And
　　Scratched Godolphin out again.
So now Godolphin is the Boy
Who blacks the Boots at the Savoy.

HILAIRE BELLOC.

Our Coronation Ode

UPLIFT thee, Muse—

*(By the way I ought to have said at once that this Ode
is going to be recited by Mrs. Banting-Bate in our
village on Coronation Day.   The Vicar asked me to
write it, and though I am not much good at poetry I
couldn't very well refuse.)*

Uplift thee, Muse, and sing us how and when
Beneath the shadow of the larger Ben
The King of England and the Queen were crowned—
With lumti-umti-umti standing round—

(I have still to put the finishing touches to my Ode, but I want to make the scheme of it public before the other poets come out with theirs : so that no one can accuse me afterwards of plagiarism.)

Uplift thee, Muse, and sing us why and where
So many what-d'you-call-'ems sit and stare
Upon the King of England and the Queen
In tooral-ooral-umti-something sheen—

(You see the idea.)

But most uplift thee, Muse, to tell of those
Who for the lack of necessary clothes,
Or else because they do not like a crush,
Remain behind at Bewdlay - on - the - Mush — *(our village).*
Their hearts beat just as loyally as if,
Clad in a something-umthing collar stiff,
Or in a lumti-tumti harem gown
They'd left the country for the stifling town.
Loyalty bursts from every heart in spates,
But, most of all, from Mr. Banting-Bate's !—

(Husband of Mrs. Banting-Bate. He has very kindly lent his hill for the bonfire. There will be a pause here, while the Vicar leads the cheering.)

Lo, lightly dawns at last the day of Kings,
Of Pomps and Power and Pageantry and things,
When to the Abbey goes beloved George—
Ter-rumti-umti-umti forge or gorge—

(This line doesn't look very promising at present.)

Archbishop, Bishop, Dean, Archdeacon, Priest,
Gathered from North and South and West and
    East,

247

Duke, Marquis, Earl, Baron and Baronet
And Viscount too, in solemn conclave met,
Salute him, England's monarch—" George the
    Fifth ! "

*(Tremendous applause, led by Mr. Banting-Bate.
I hope it will go on long enough to hide the fact that
we are going to lose a line here. The fact is there is
simply no rhyme to " fifth."*

And lo, the cheers break forth, both long and loud,
From everybody in the Abbey's crowd—
From Duke and Deacon, from the *Daily Mail's*
Own correspondent and the Prince of Wales.
Still more they cheer (how much I cannot tell)
As soon as good Queen Mary's crowned as well—

*(Applause led by Mrs. Bletherstone, who inaugurated
the Mary Fund in our village.)*

The ceremony over, then they go
Around the city in procession slow ;
In all the pageantry of pomp and power
They ride through London for about an hour—
    (roughly)
Let us, dear people, let us leave them there—
So kingly, queenly, noble and so fair.

*(A pause, while Miss Gathers of the Post Office
presents Mrs. Banting-Bate with a glass of water.)*

So much for that. And now a solemn hush
Comes o'er us here in Bewdlay-on-the-Mush.
These scenes which I have tried to adumbrate—
The Coronation and the March in State—
These scenes are not for us—except, I hope,
Upon the Little Bewdlay bioscope.

But even here, remote from King and Queen,
How great our preparat-i-ons have been!
Some say the tale of it has darkly spread
From Upper Bewdlay down to Bewdlay Head—

(*Two important towns in the neighbourhood.*)

Who knows but what a rumour of the thing
Has even reached our gracious Queen and King!
How that a certain resident of fame—(*Mr. Banting-*
Bate)
Has nobly lent the place which bears his name—

(*Banting Place. Mr. Bate took the additional name*
of Banting when he took the place. And, to be exact,
he has only lent one hill on the Estate.)

That there a bonfire might be built and burnt
And lessons too of loyalty be learnt—

(*I mean, of course, that the bonfire will in itself be*
a lesson. Not that any sort of continuation class will
be held upon the ashes.)

Moreover, how the Vicar will assist
Supported by his kindly wife, I wist—

(*Not good—and might easily be misinterpreted.*
Will alter.)

When all the children each receive a mug
Designed by Mrs. Welkington (*née* Sugg)—

(*An extraordinary bit of luck. I don't know what I*
should have done for a rhyme otherwise.)

Next, Muse, take out thy lyre and sing the song
Short-long, short-long, short-long, short-long, short-
long—

(A difficulty here being that the rest of the celebrations are not yet decided upon. However, I anticipate no trouble when once the facts are in my hands.)

*   *   *

Now let us turn our thoughts across the sea
To where the Union Jack is waving free !
I breathe upon my magic harp and sing
The what's-its-name of what-d'you-call-the-thing—

(I want a good phrase for Empire.)

For lo ! ter-umti-tooral-ooral-ay—

(This part is all a little in the rough at present. When polished up it will take up about ten lines. After that it will finish up quite quickly like this),

And now, good people, one thing still remains
Ere we go out into the fields and lanes ;
One thing before we leave this solemn scene—
Namely to cry " God Save the King and Queen ! "

A. A. MILNE.

The Proletariat

I WAS playing darts in the old " Blue Dragon " ;
    There was young Bert Baxter and a little friend
        of Jane's, Harriet and Albert, that works on
        the railway,
    And old Bill Mortimer that works upon the drains,
When up jumps a lunatic and starts a little chat,
And he calls us " Members of the Proletariat " !
        Oh, we DID laugh !
        Oh, we DID laugh !
        Ha ! Ha ! Ha !

Well, it knocks a fellow flat!
And I said, " Well, boys, what d'you think of that ?
Fancy me a Member of the Proletariat !
       Fancy me and you,
        And Harriet and Hugh,
All these years, boys, and, Lord, we never knew
We was all life-members of the Proletariat,
    The Proly-oly-roly-poly-proly-tari-at !

Well, I said, " Long words never lined a bread-box,
  But a nice long word is a comfort all the same ;
You can say what you like about the language of
    Shakespeare,
  But this here mouthful puts the man to shame ;
For you do feel good, and there's no denying that,
If you speak about a plumber as the Proletariat ! "
       Oh, we DID *laugh !*
       Oh, we DID *laugh !*
       Ha ! Ha ! Ha !
  Well, it knocks a fellow flat !
And Bill said, firm-like, he didn't mean to be
Not an economic pawn, nor a bond-slave—see ?
      So I held Nell's hand,
      And we all felt grand,
And we gave three cheers for to Socialize the Land
And we took a season-ticket for the Proletariat,
    The Proly-oly-roly-poly-proly-tari-at !

Then I went out, and I said to a policeman,
  " Comrade, wage-slave, ain't it very strange,
These here capitalists don't want to nationalize
  The Means of Production, Distribution and
    Exchange ?
If you ask me, Constable, I'm taking off my hat
To the Nancimancipation of the Proletariat ! "

> Oh, he DID laugh!
> Oh, he DID laugh!
> Ha! Ha! Ha!
> Well, it knocks a fellow flat!
> So he said, kind-like, " Come along of me! "
> But I said, " What about Solidaritee? "
> And Bill said, " Shame!
> Solidarity's the game! "
> But he took me off to the station just the same,
> Though we're both life-members of the Proletariat,
> The Proly-oly-roly-poly-proly-tari-at!
>
> A. P. HERBERT.

Mr. Jones

" THERE's been an accident," they said,
" Your servant's cut in half; he's dead! "
" Indeed! " said Mr. Jones, " and please
Send me the half that's got my keys."

CAPTAIN HARRY GRAHAM.

The Passing of the Strange Guest

AT the Gargoyle Hotel, Aberglidden,
A Guest went suddenly mad.
The Gargoyle Hotel, Aberglidden,
Is famed for its Scenic Environs
And famed for its Perfect Cuisine,
It is centrally heated throughout:
Yet No. 140
Having given a tip to the Porter,
And given a tip to the Boots,
And given a tip to the Chambermaid,
And given a tip to his Waiter,

And a tip to the Principal Waiter,
And the Waiter who brought him his Wine ;
Such Wine !
And a tip to the Man at the Garage,
And a tip to one or two Pages,
And a tip to Heaven knows whom,
Being poised, as it were, at the Portal
About to depart
Went suddenly back to the Office,

Ah me !
And asked them to kindly oblige him
With Change for a Ten-Pound Note,
Which he took in Small Pieces of Silver,
And then——
None daring to thwart or gainsay him,
So Dark was his Mood——
Ranged through the Hotel like a Viking
And tipped, not regarding their Stations,
All Persons who stood in his way.
The two Millionaires from Chicago
And the Wives of the two Millionaires
He tipped,
And a Prosperous Lady from Bootle,
From Bootle in Lancs,
And a Lady of Seventy Summers
Whose Father had been a Q.C.,
And also the Chef,
Who had come up to talk to a Waiter,
And a Colonel grown fiery with Golfing,
And a golden-haired Damsel or twain,

The Old, the Infirm, and the Youthful,
Both Young Men and Maidens
Tipped he them.

Till they called in the end the Proprietor
Who came looking Tactfully stern,
But No. 140
Not staying his hand
Put a Two-Shilling Piece in the Waistcoat,
The beautiful bow-fronted Waistcoat
With vest-slip complete
That the goodly Proprietor wore :
And THEN
Having noticed at last near the Entrance
A huge Stuffed Bear
Which was Standing Erect on its Hind Legs
And holding a Tray,
He gave what was left of his Largesse
To that. . . .
So passed, but not all unforgotten,
From the Gargoyle Hotel, Aberglidden,
Having solved the Gratuity Problem,
The Curious Guest.

E. V. KNOX.

A TAIL-PIECE

Ad Lectionem Suam

WHEN Autumn's winds denude the grove,
  I seek my Lecture, where it lurks
'Mid the unpublished portion of
        My works,

And ponder, while its sheets I scan,
  How many years away have slipt
Since first I penned that ancient man-
        uscript.

I know thee well—nor can mistake
  The old accustomed pencil stroke
Denoting where I mostly make
        A joke,—

Or where coy brackets signify
  Those echoes faint of classic wit
Which, if a lady's present, I
        Omit.

Though Truth enlarge her widening range,
  And Knowledge be with time increased,
While thou, my Lecture! dost not change
        The least,

But fixed immutable amidst
  The advent of a newer lore
Maintainest calmly what thou didst
        Before :

Though still malignity avows
  That unsuccessful candidates
To thee ascribe their frequent ploughs
        In Greats—

Once more for intellectual food
   Thou'lt serve : an added phrase or two
Will make thee really just as good
      As new.

And listening crowds, that throng the spot,
   Will still as usual complain
That " Here's the old familiar rot
      Again ! "

A. D. GODLEY.

Index of Authors

    260

261

Index of Titles

265

Printed in Great Britain by Butler & Tanner Ltd., Frome and London